Taro Gomi was born in Tokyo in 1945. In his very long career, he has created more than 350 books for readers of all ages. His work has been translated into more than 15 languages, and among the 30 of his books to be published outside of Japan are **Everyone Poops, My Friends, Spring Is Here,** and **Scribbles.**

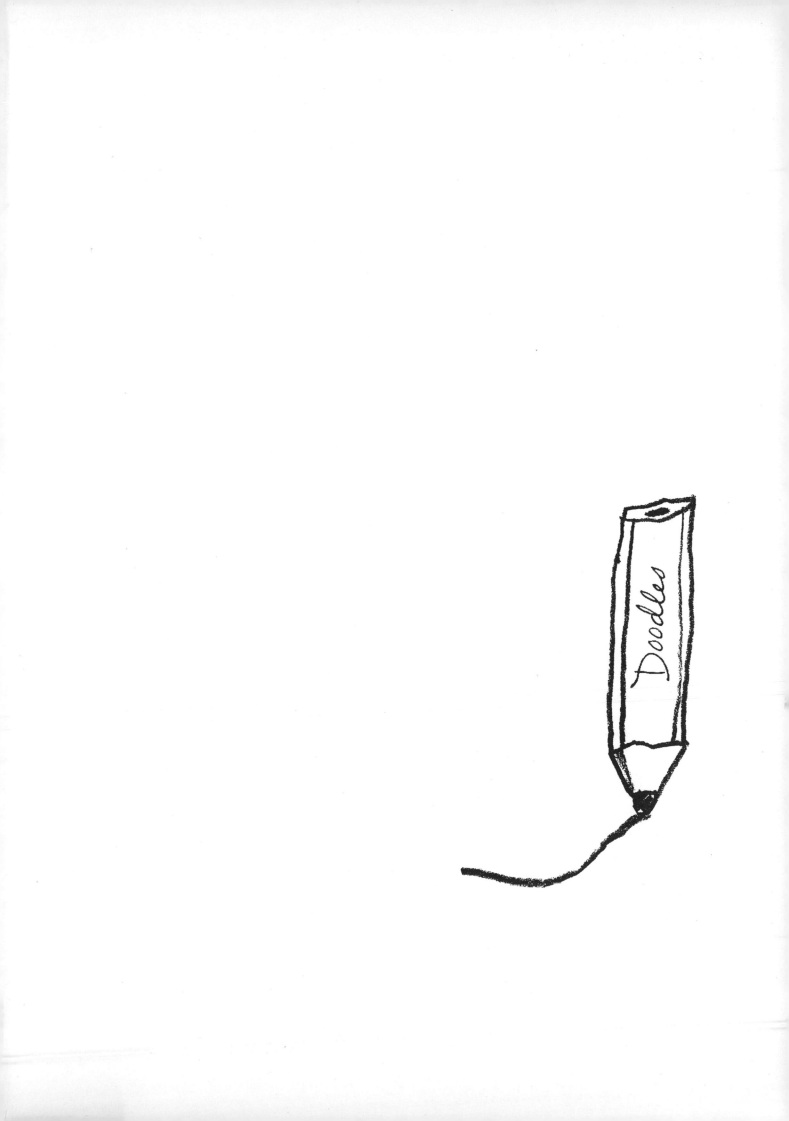

First published in the United States in 2006 by Chronicle Books LLC.

Originally published in Japan in 1992 by Bronze Publishing Inc.
under the title *Rakugaki Ehon, Part 2*.
Published by arrangement with Bronze Publishing Inc, Tokyo,
through Future View Technology Ltd.

Translation by Shoshanna Kirk.
English type design by Brenden Mendoza.
Typeset in Super Grotesk.
Manufactured by Tien Wah Press, Singapore, in July 2010.

ISBN-10 0-8118-5250-4
ISBN-13 978-0-8118-5250-0

10 9 8 7 6 5

This Product conforms to CPSIA 2008.

Chronicle Books LLC
680 Second Street, San Francisco, California 94107

www.chroniclekids.com

Doodles

Really Giant

A Coloring and
Doodling Book

Taro
Gomi

chronicle books · san francisco

It's a tug-of-war. Draw the rest of the team.

(No fair drawing a bulldozer!)

Fill these glasses with your favorite ice cream.

The most mouthwatering wins!

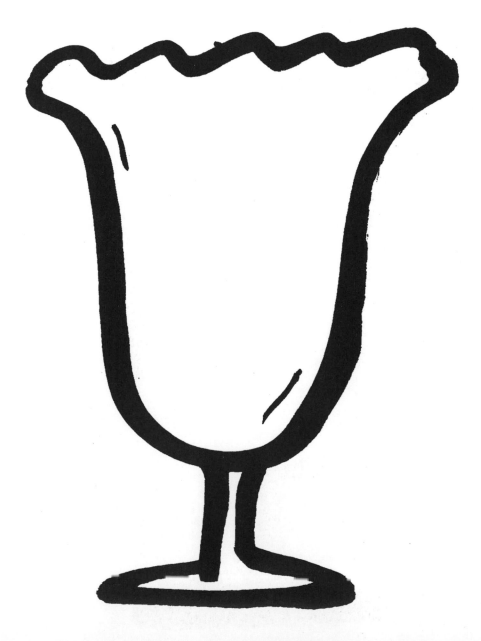

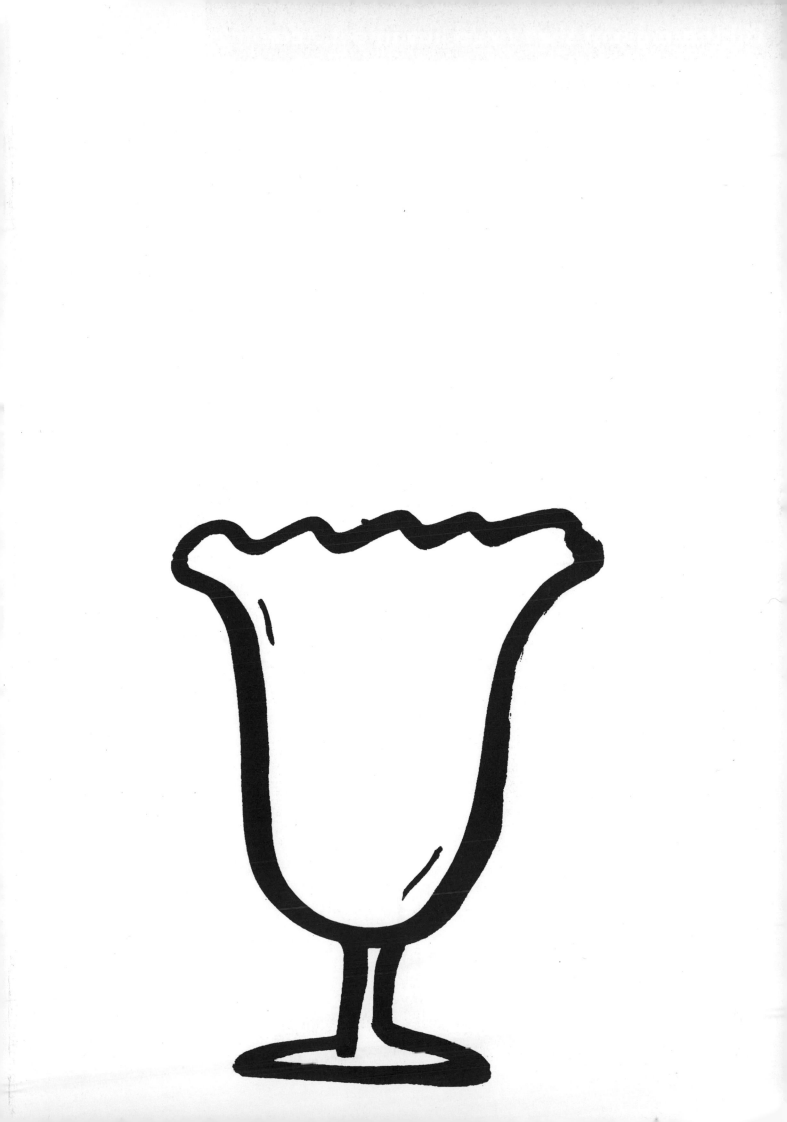

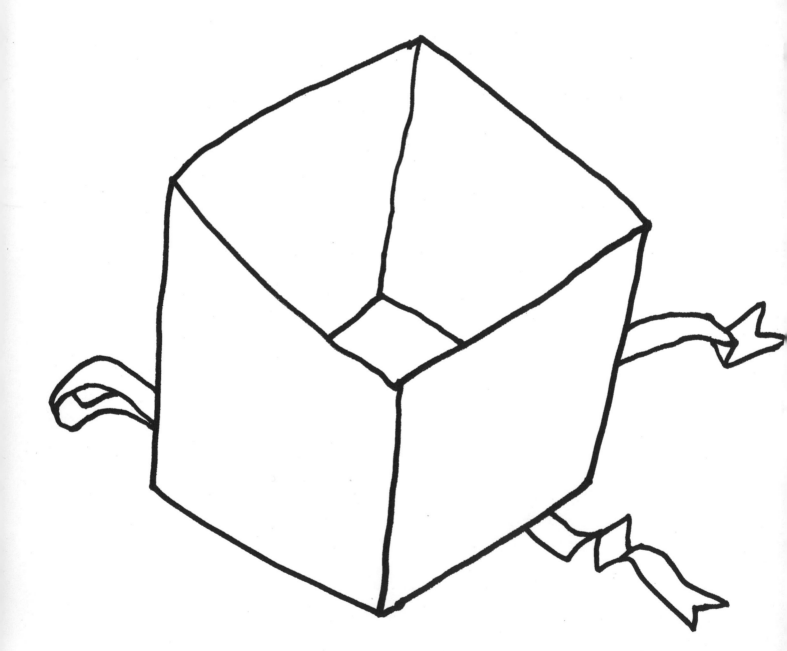

Give them arms and legs and imagine that they're having a battle.

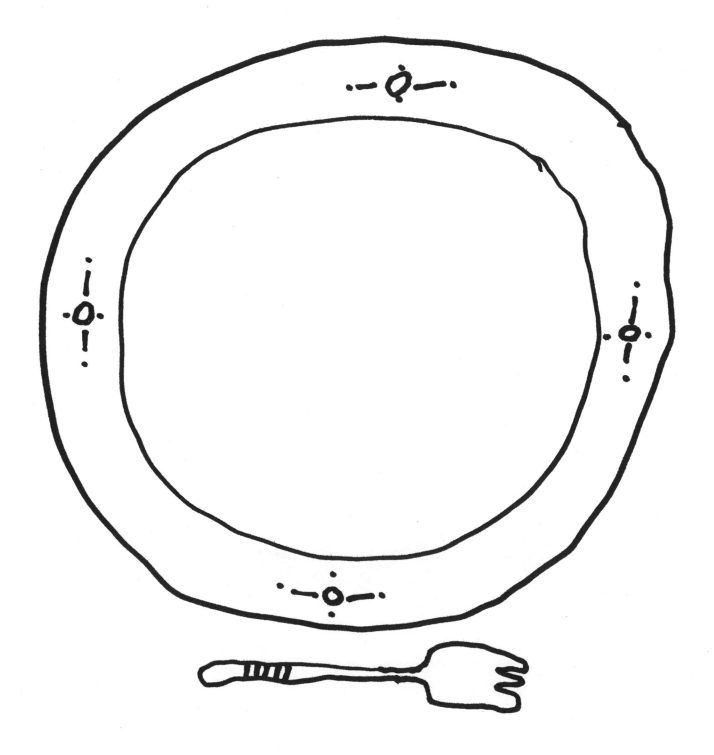

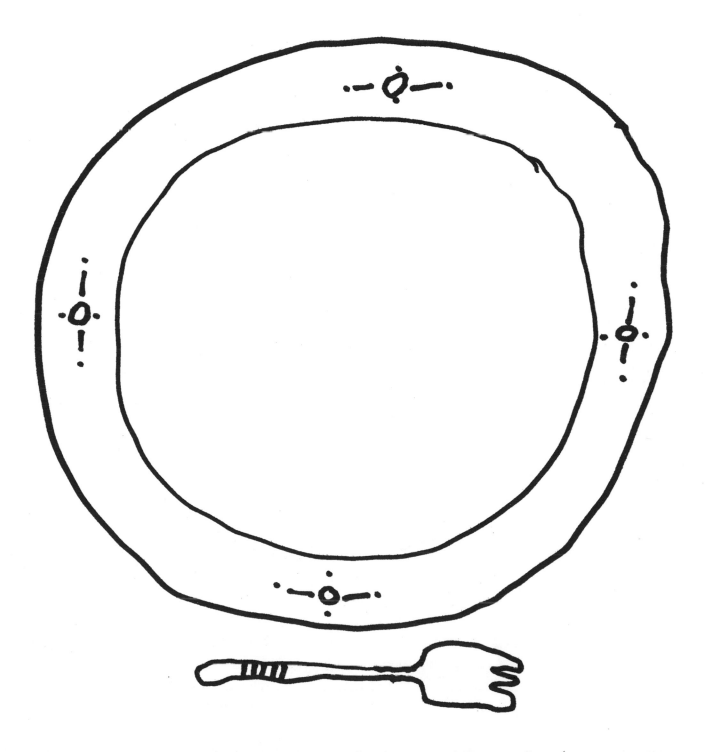

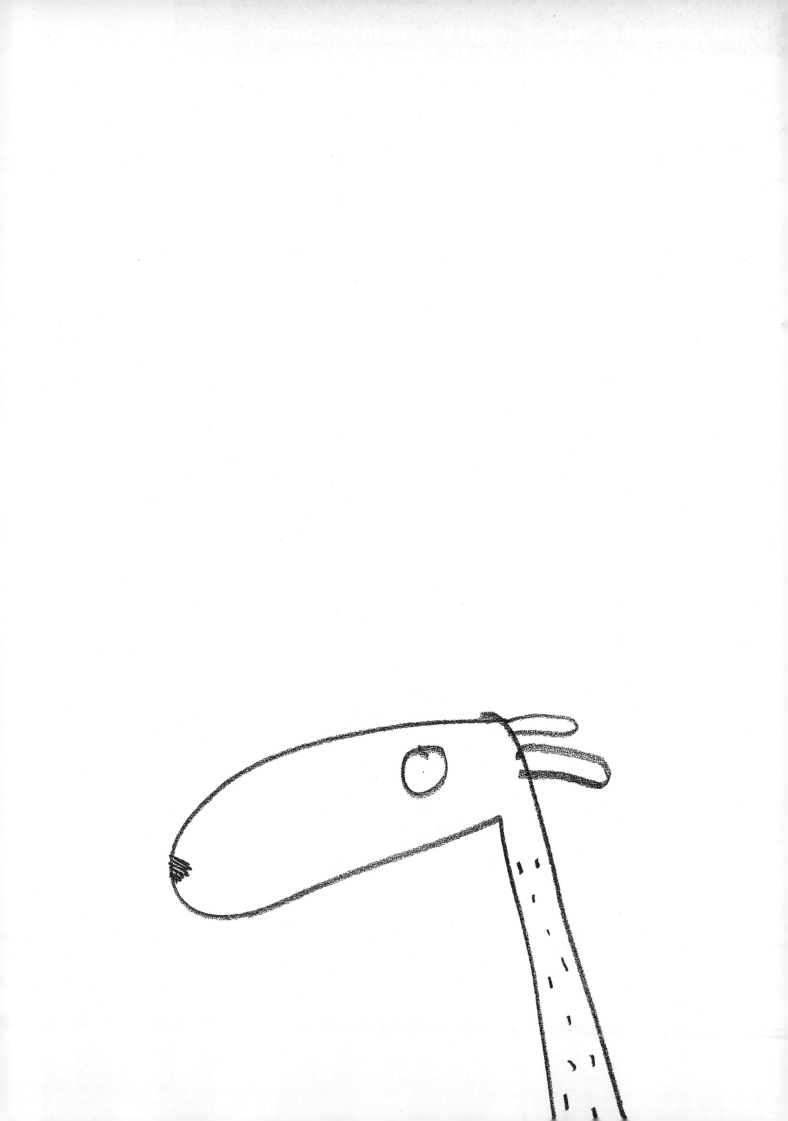

Spring has arrived. Imagine what might be sprouting.

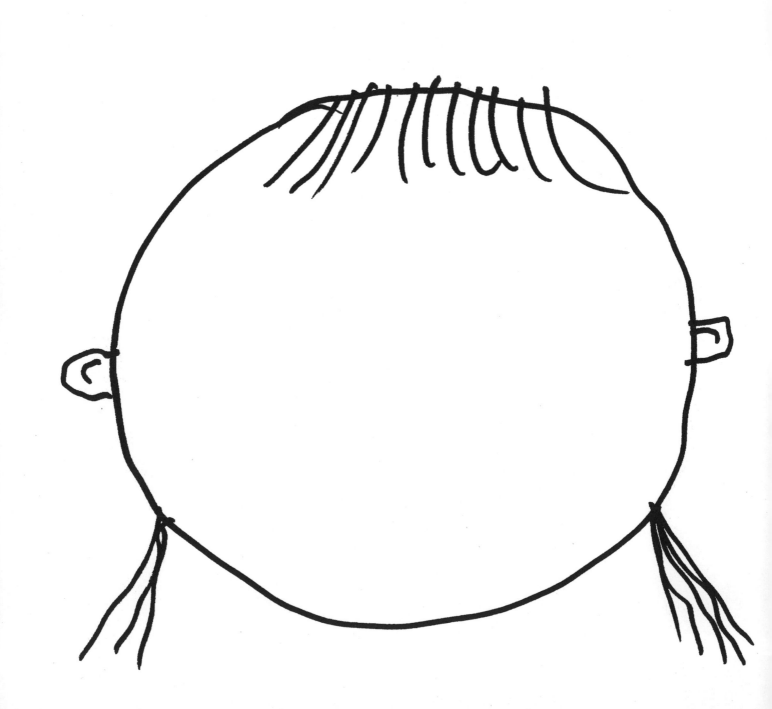

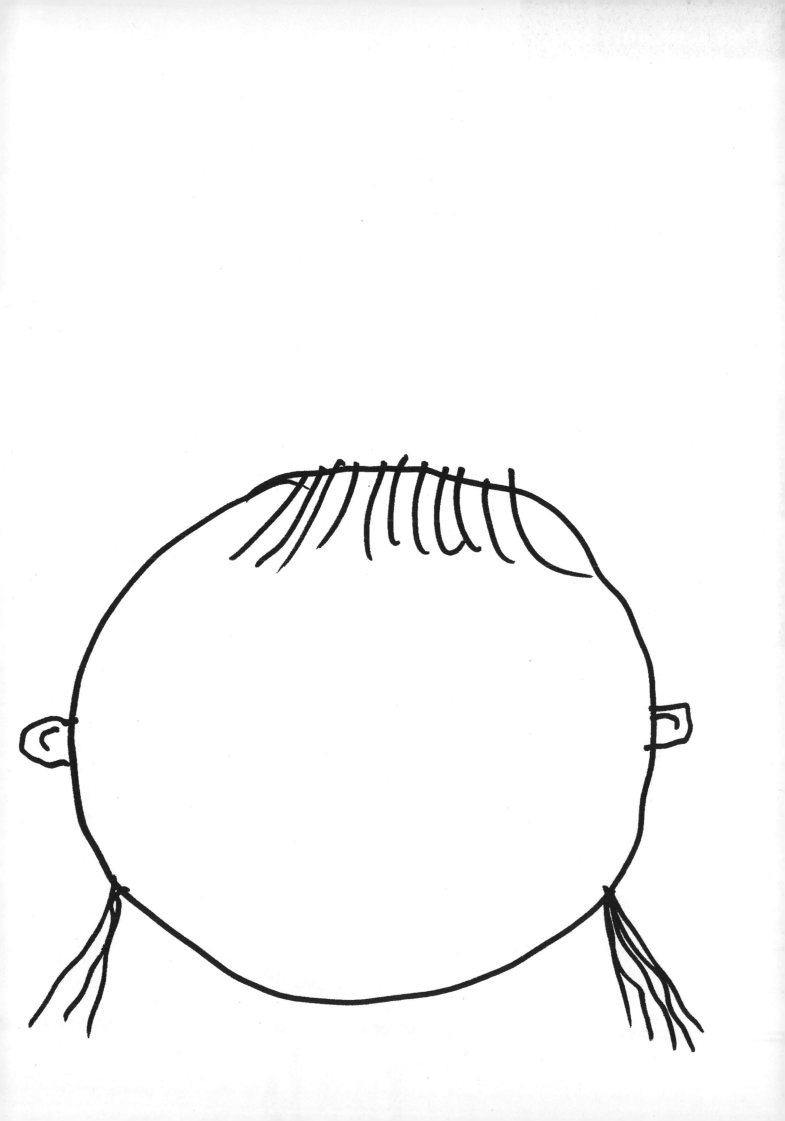

Design the flag of the country of rabbits.
And the flag of the country of mice.

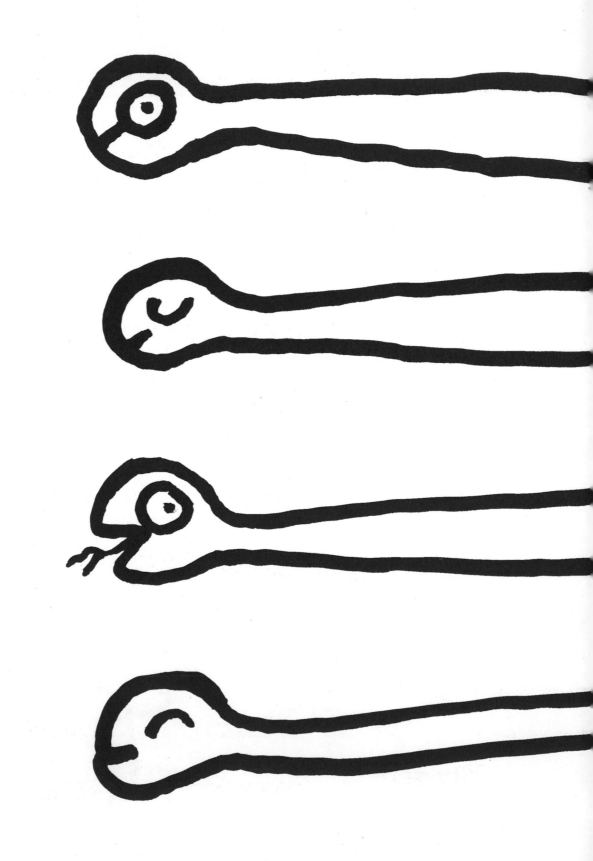

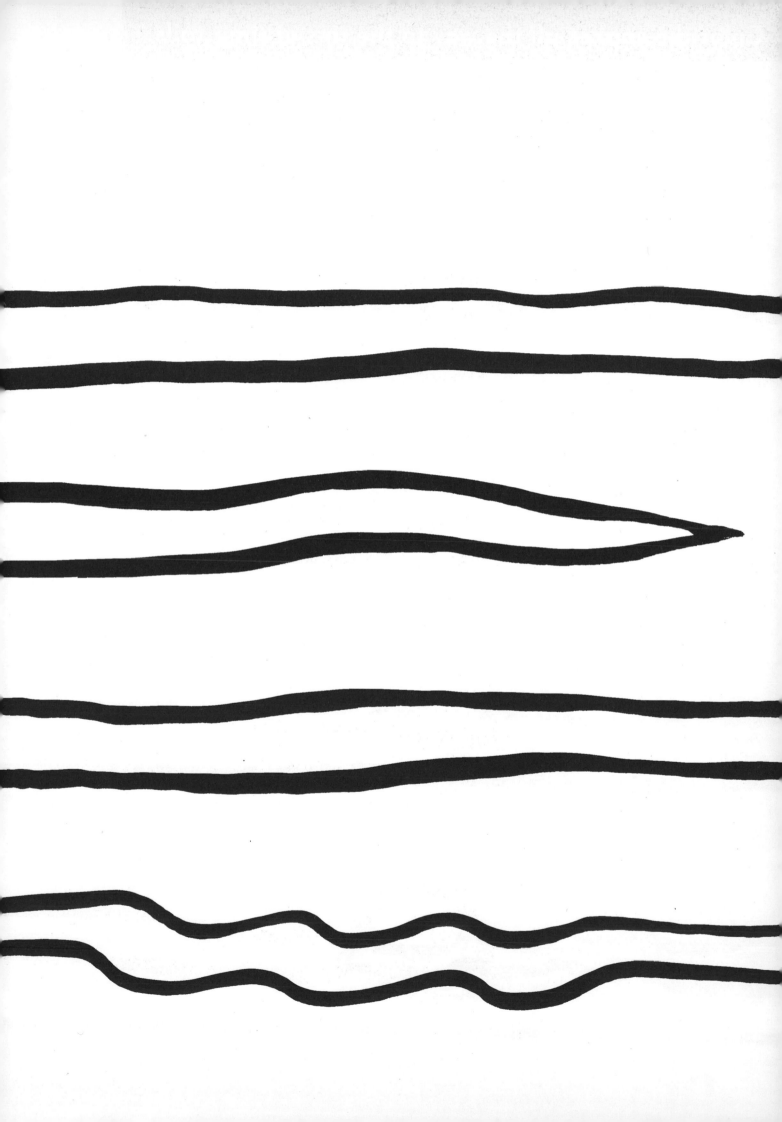

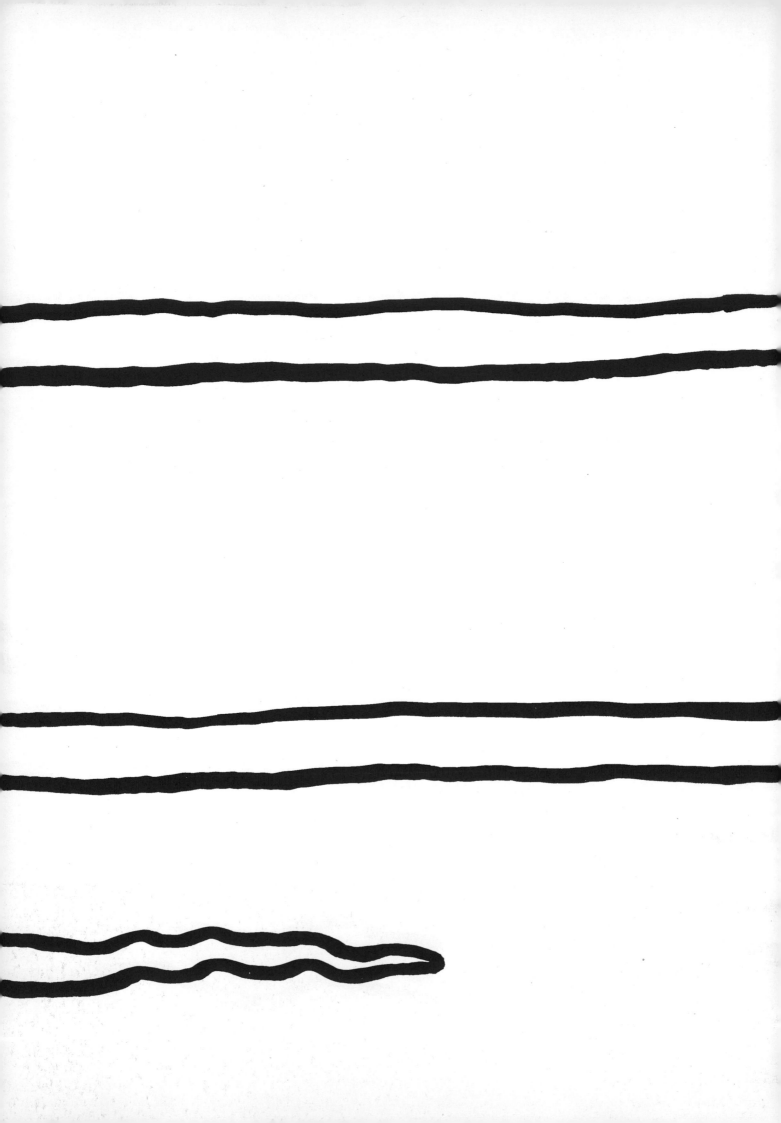

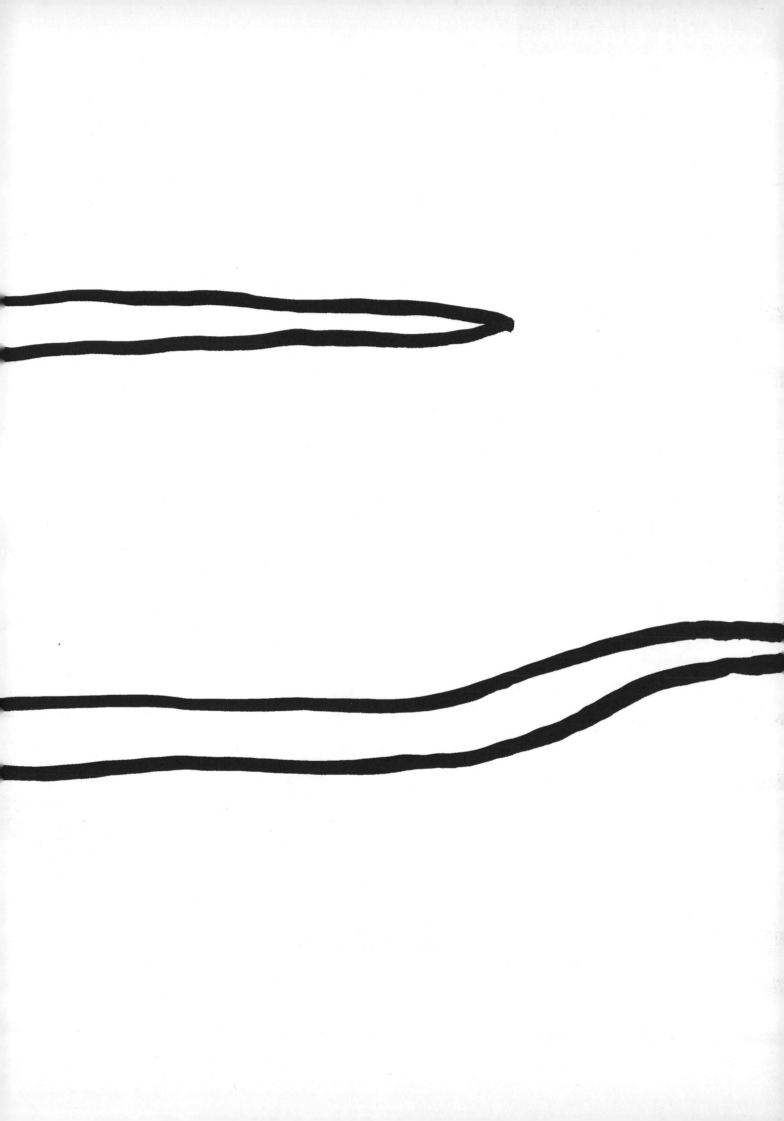

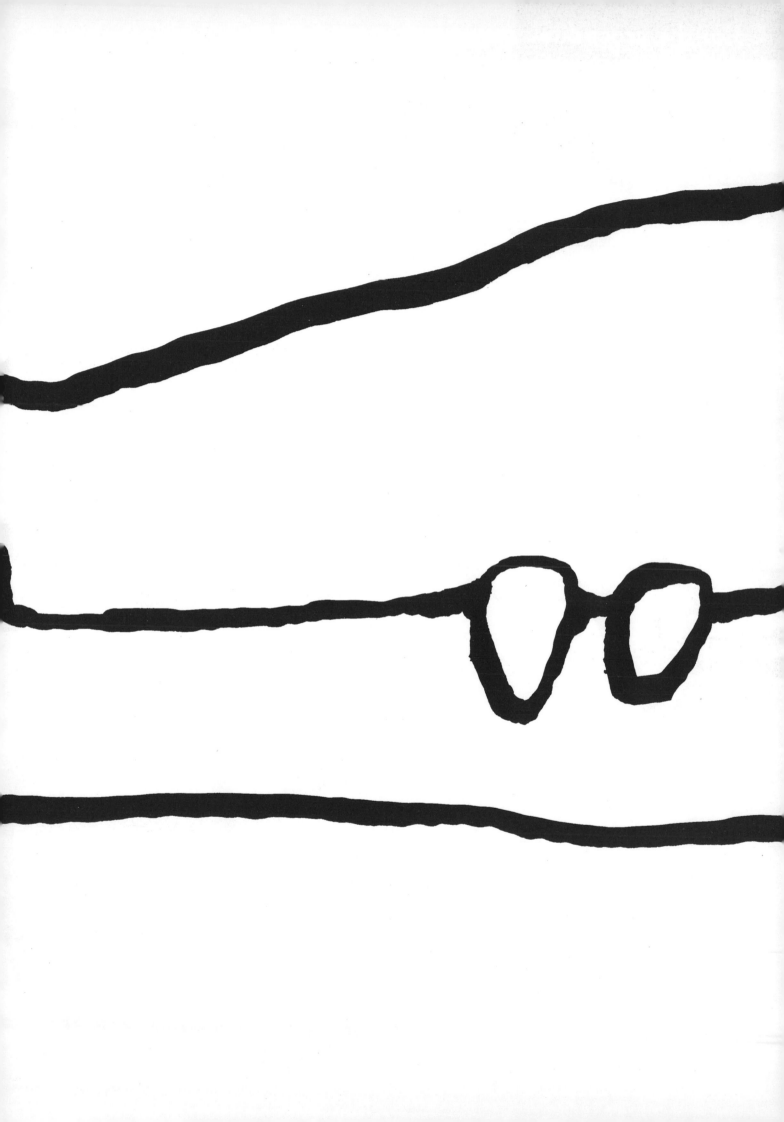

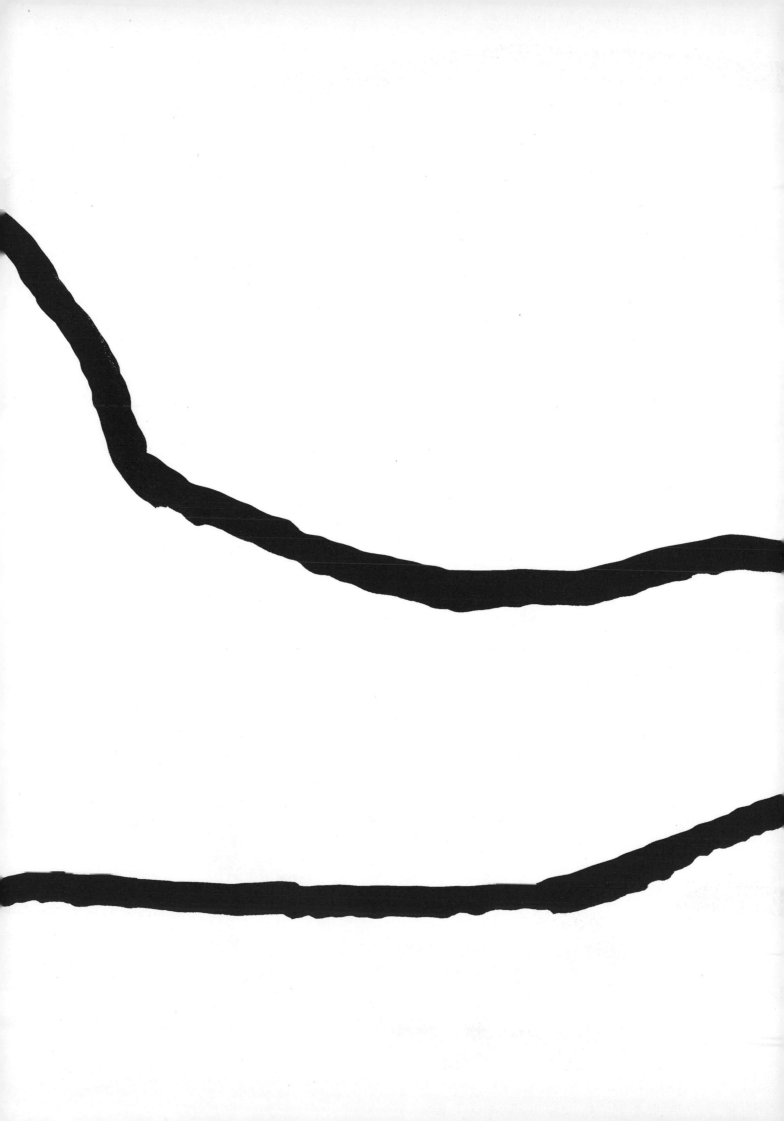

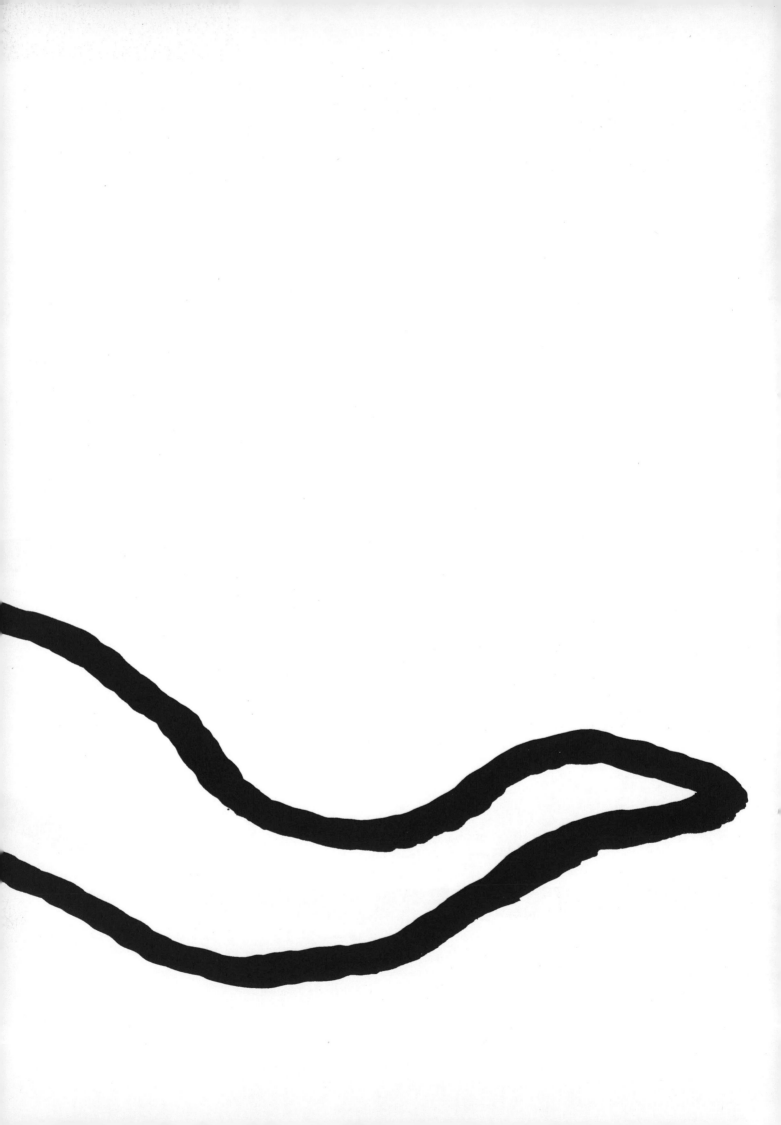

(If it were the same scale as the crocodile, it would be 42 pages long! So I had to make it a little smaller.)

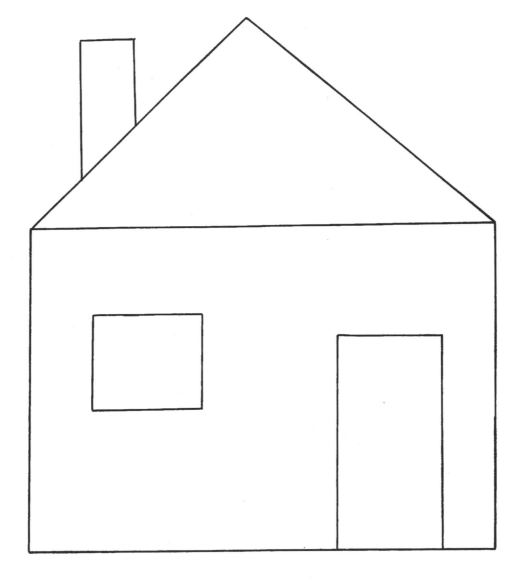

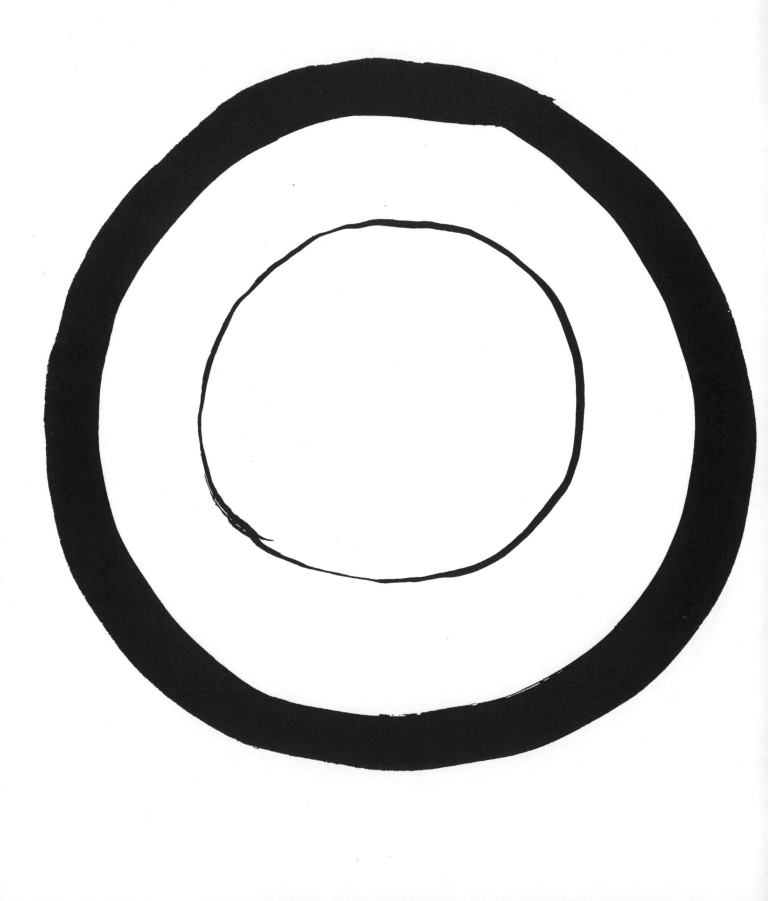

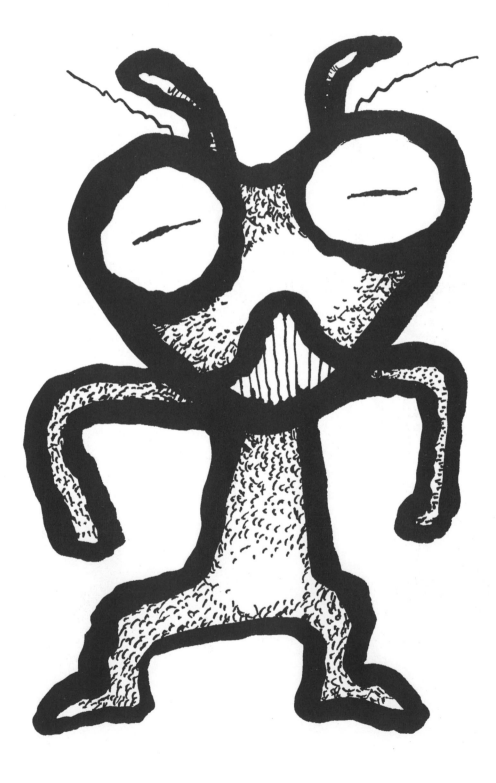

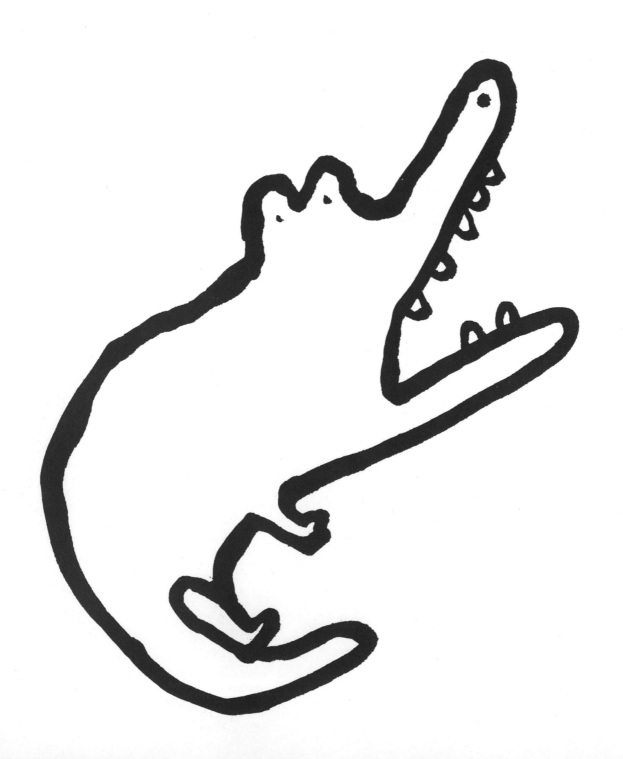

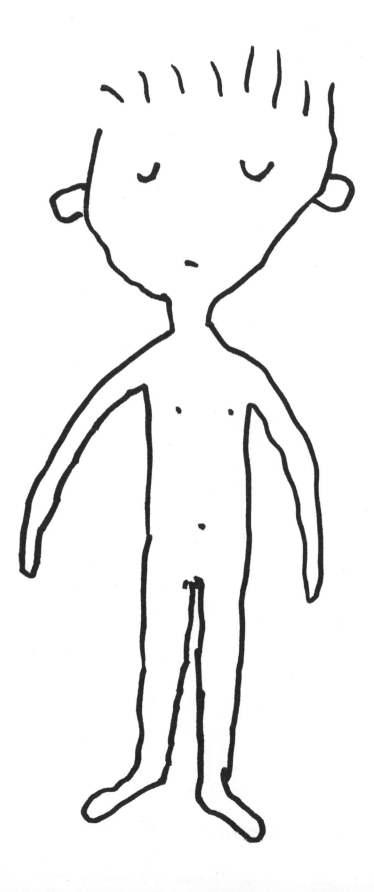

(You could put sunglasses on them, for example.)

These elephants have a problem. What is it?

Here are two shops.
Draw signs and things to buy.

Also draw shoppers.

This is a neon sign.
Color the squares so that the word **sea** appears.

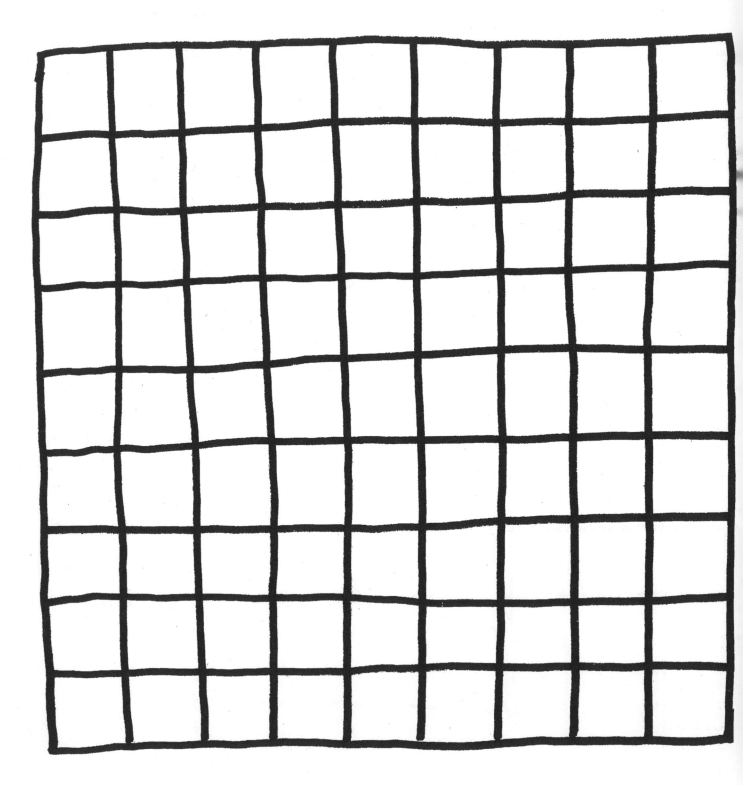

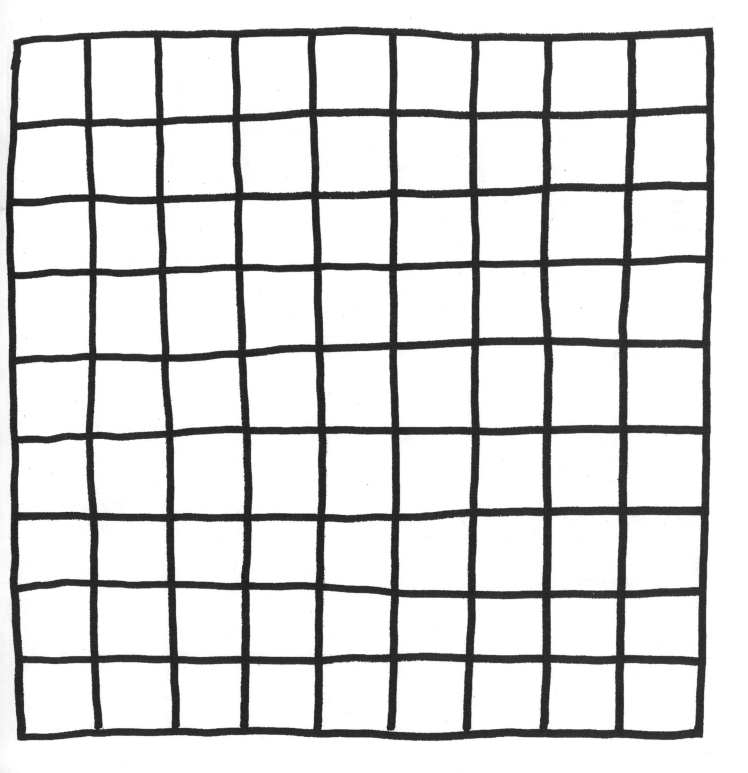

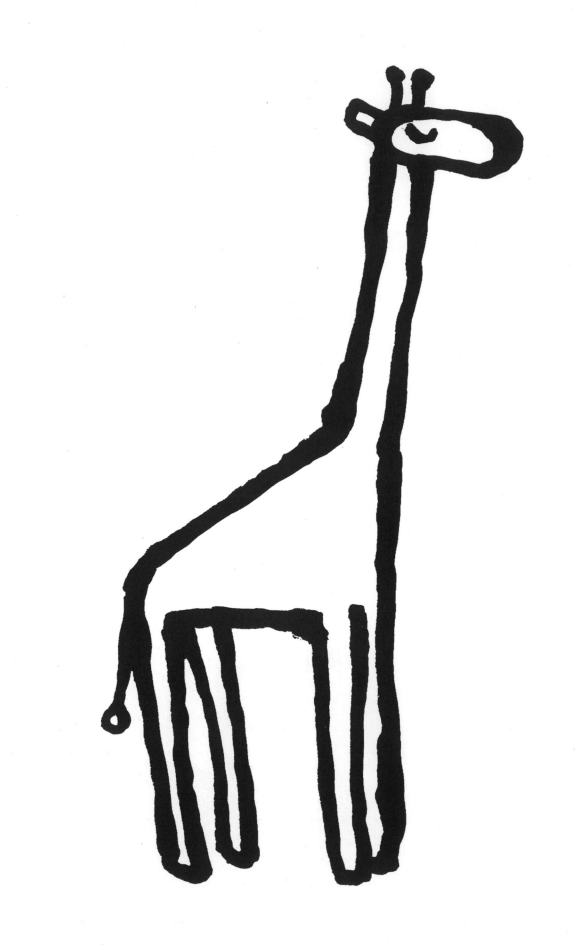

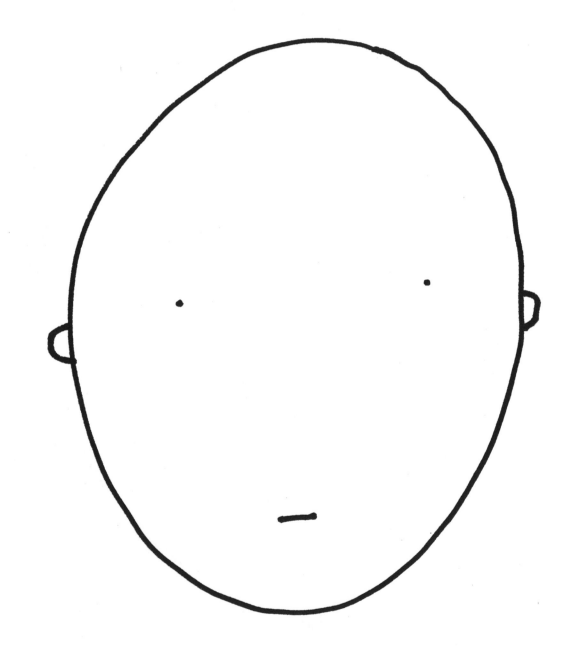

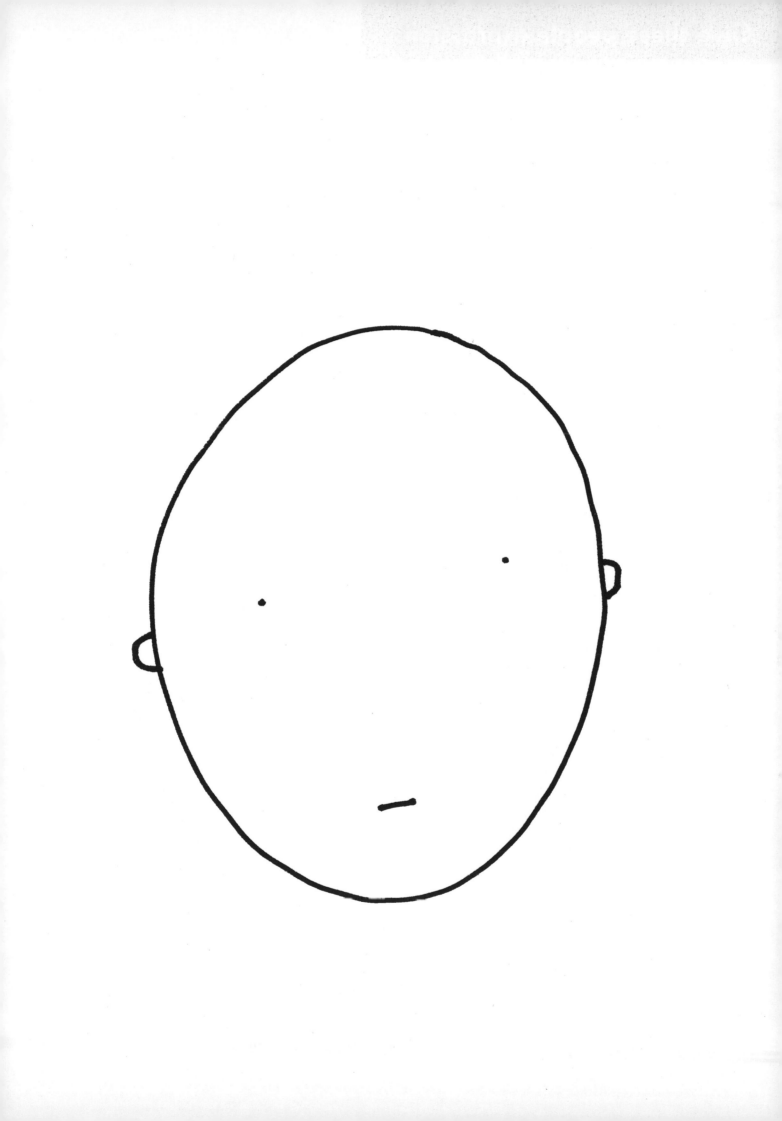

You can make up names for their teams.

**This is a little ten-page book.
You get to make up the story.**

Don't forget to give it a title!

by: _____
illustrations by Taro Gomi

published by Doodles Books

isbn: 0-8118-1881-0
Doodles Books
$18.95

This is the back cover.
Cut out the pages and make it into a real book.

If you're really proud of your book,
you can send it to:

Doodles
c/o Chronicle Kids Books
85 Second Street, 6th floor
San Francisco, CA 94105

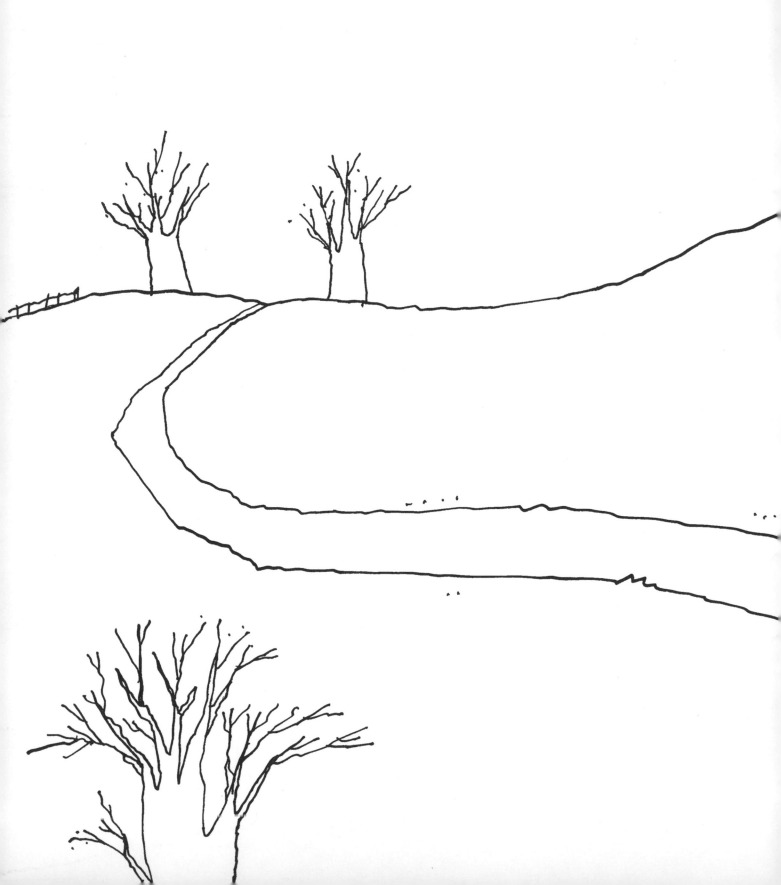

Spring is here.
Color this landscape with spring colors.

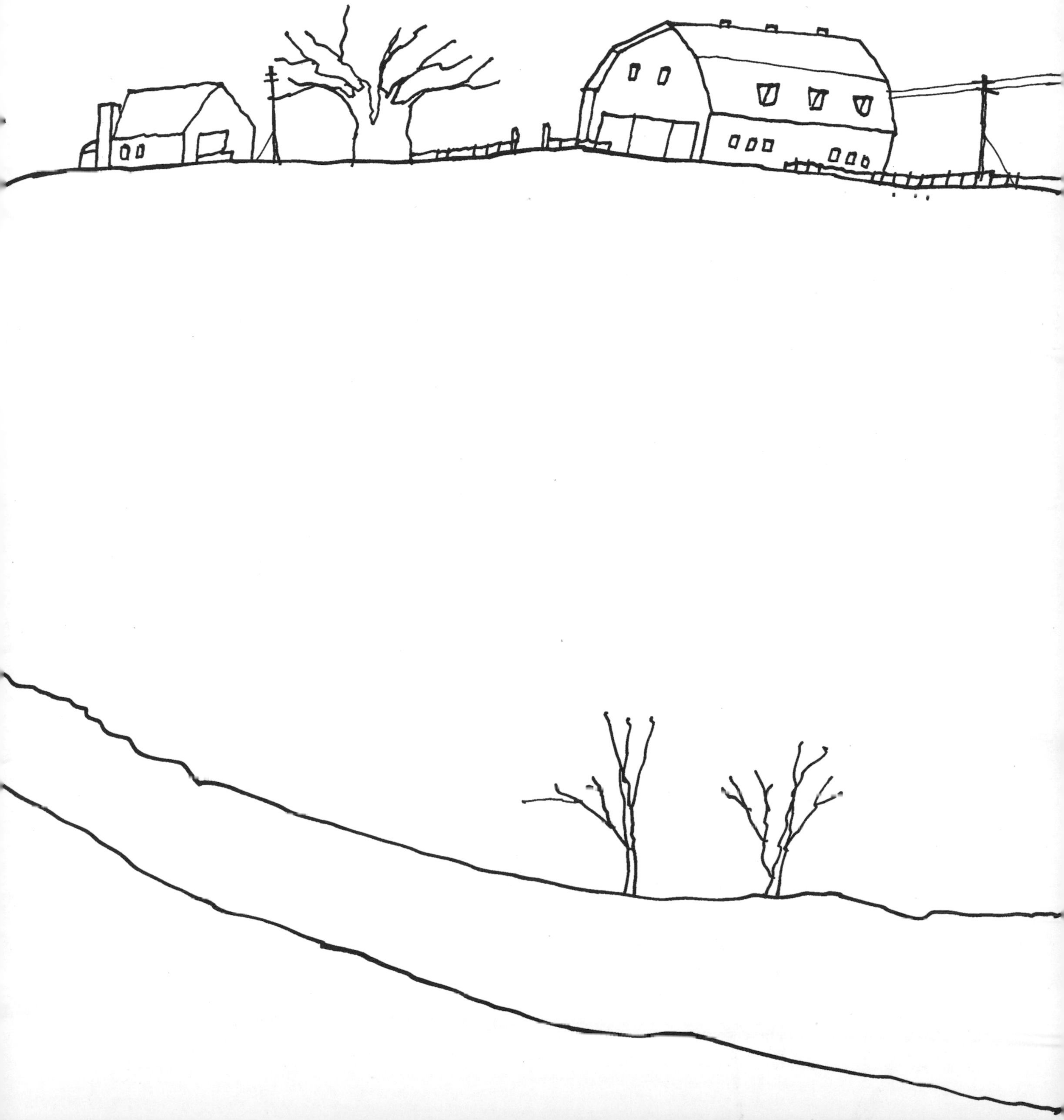

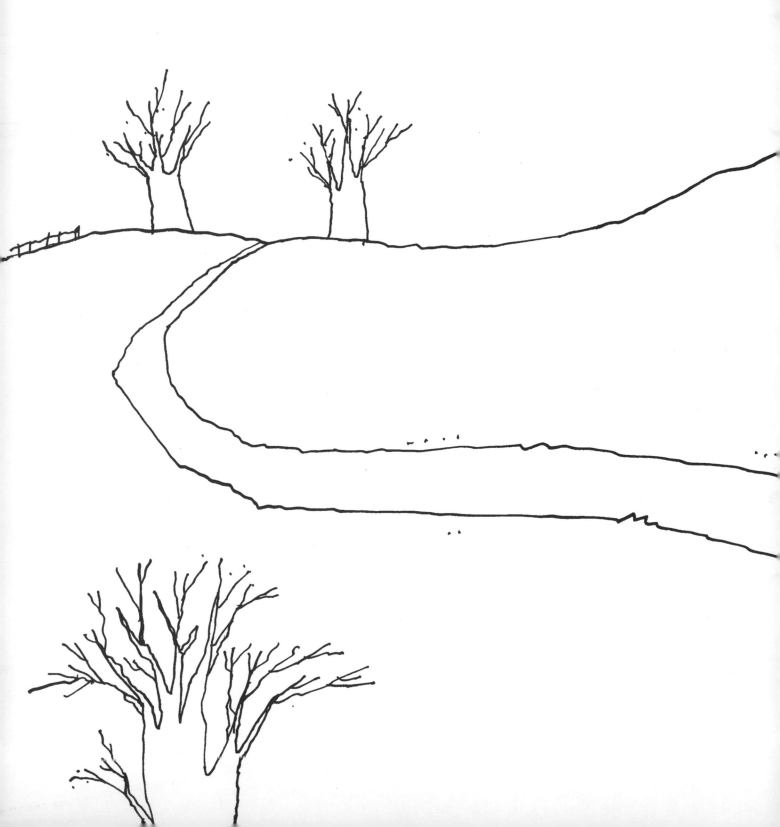

**Summer is here.
Draw a summery landscape.**

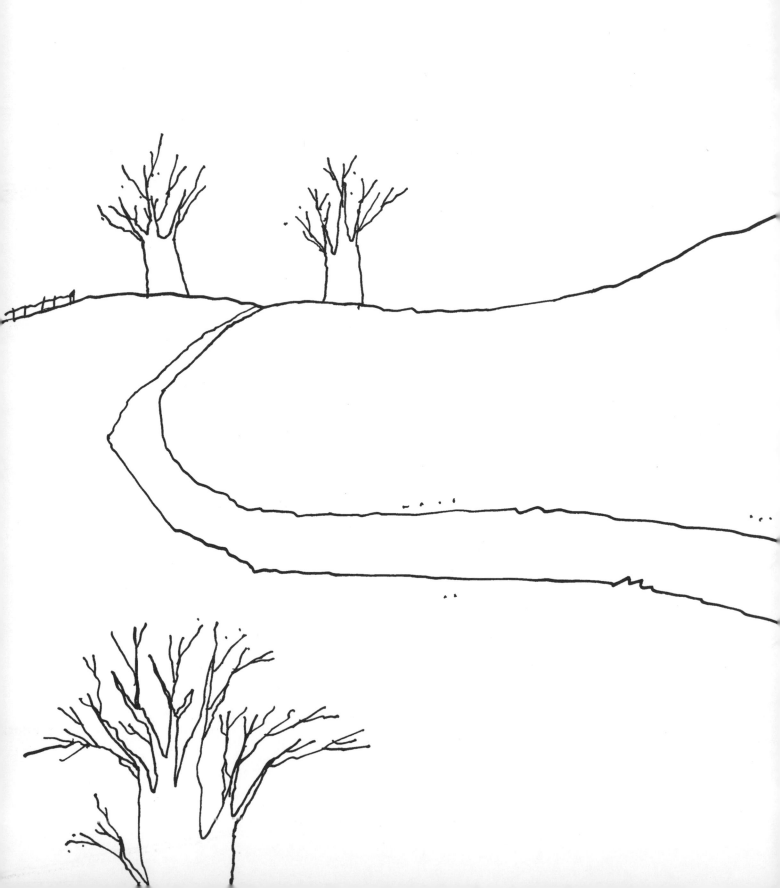

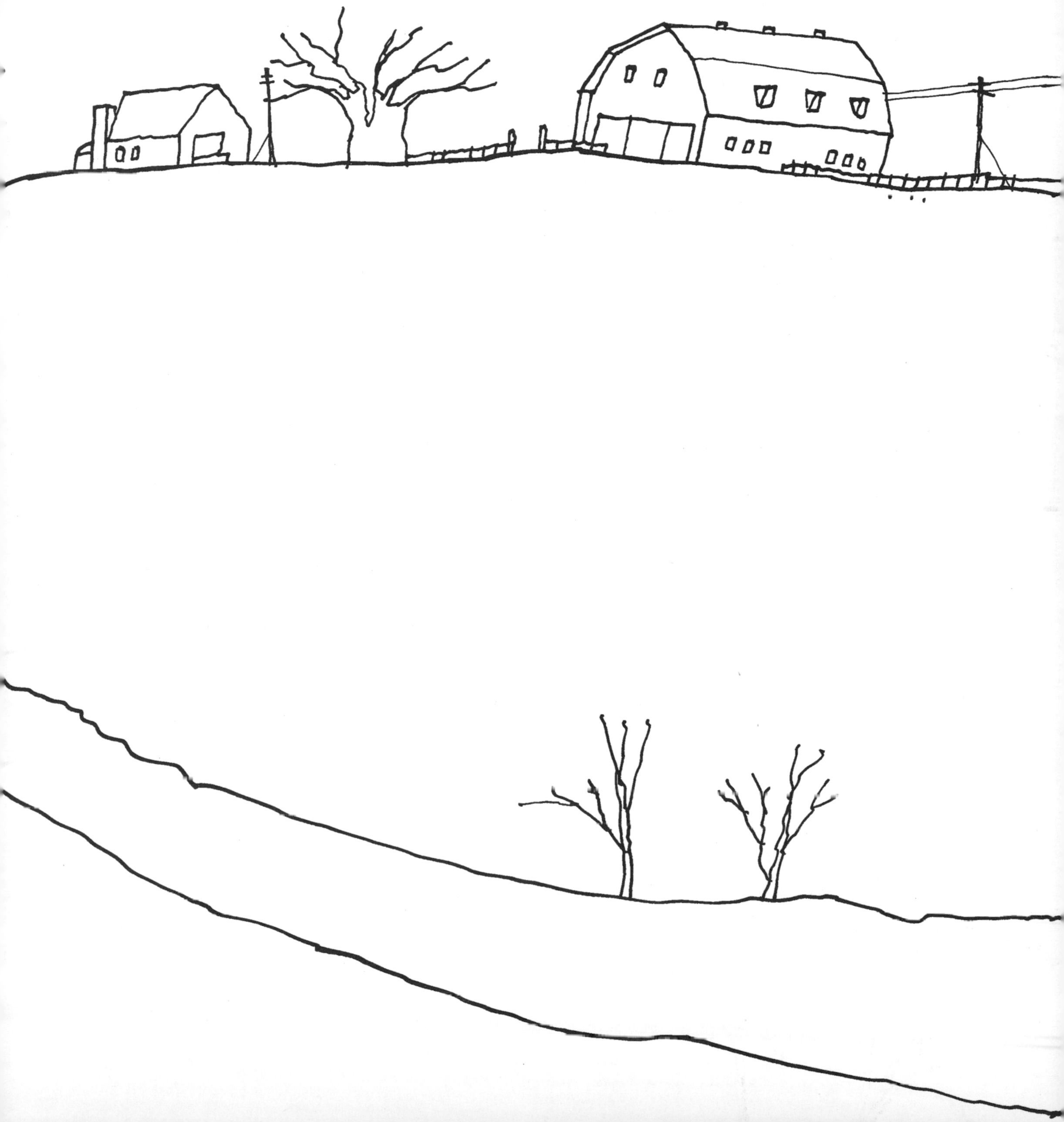

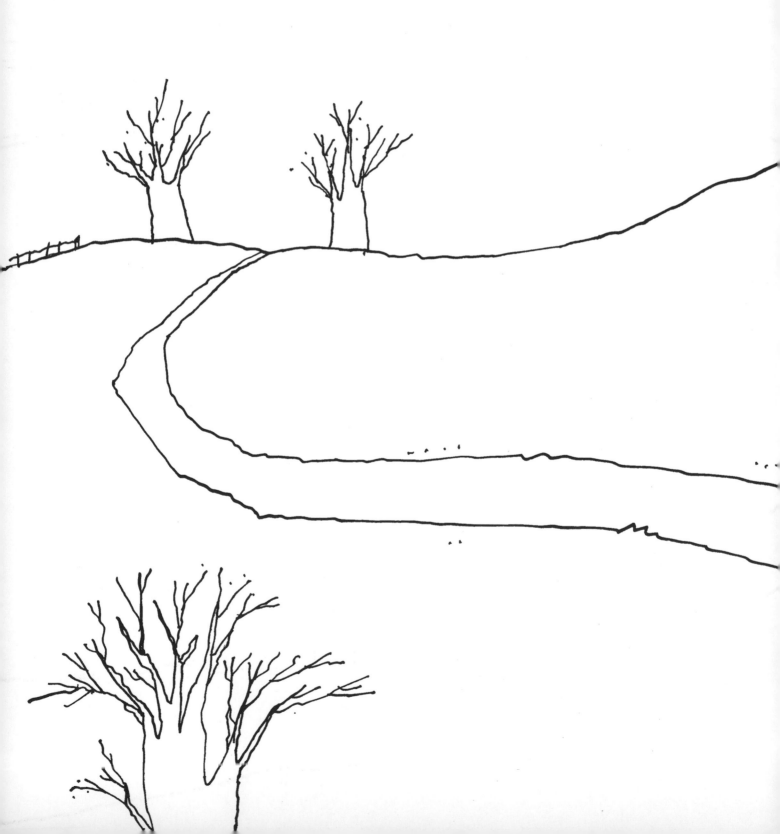

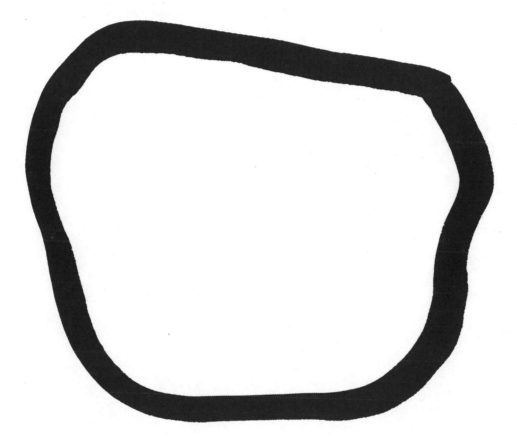

Make them have a snowball fight.

Draw something whose name begins with the last letter of the thing before it.

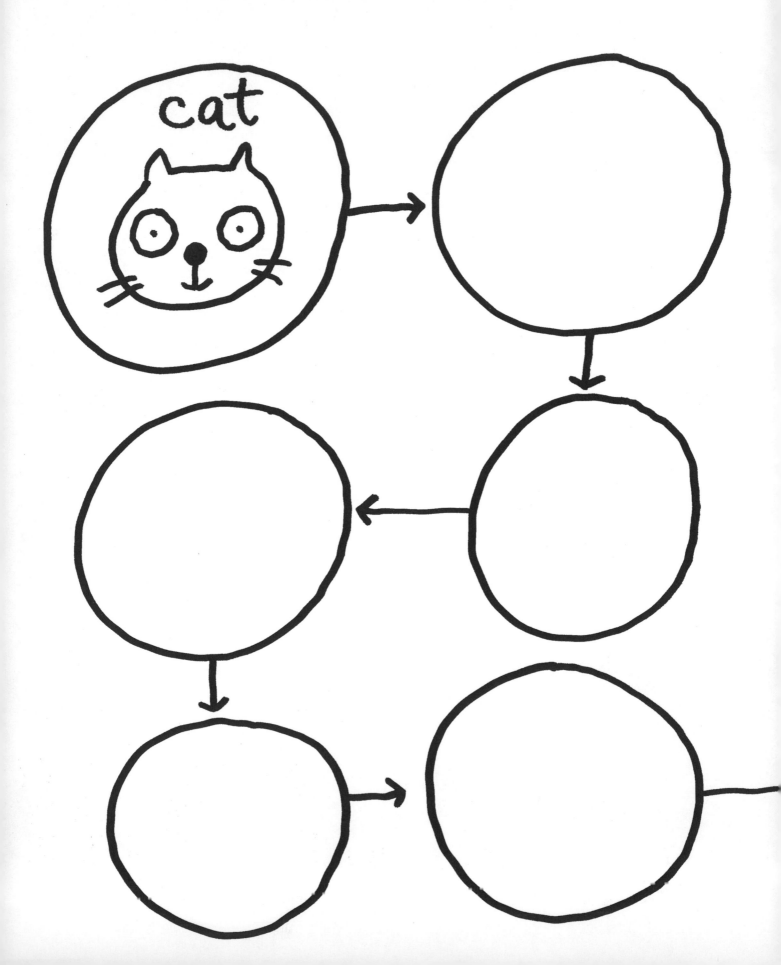

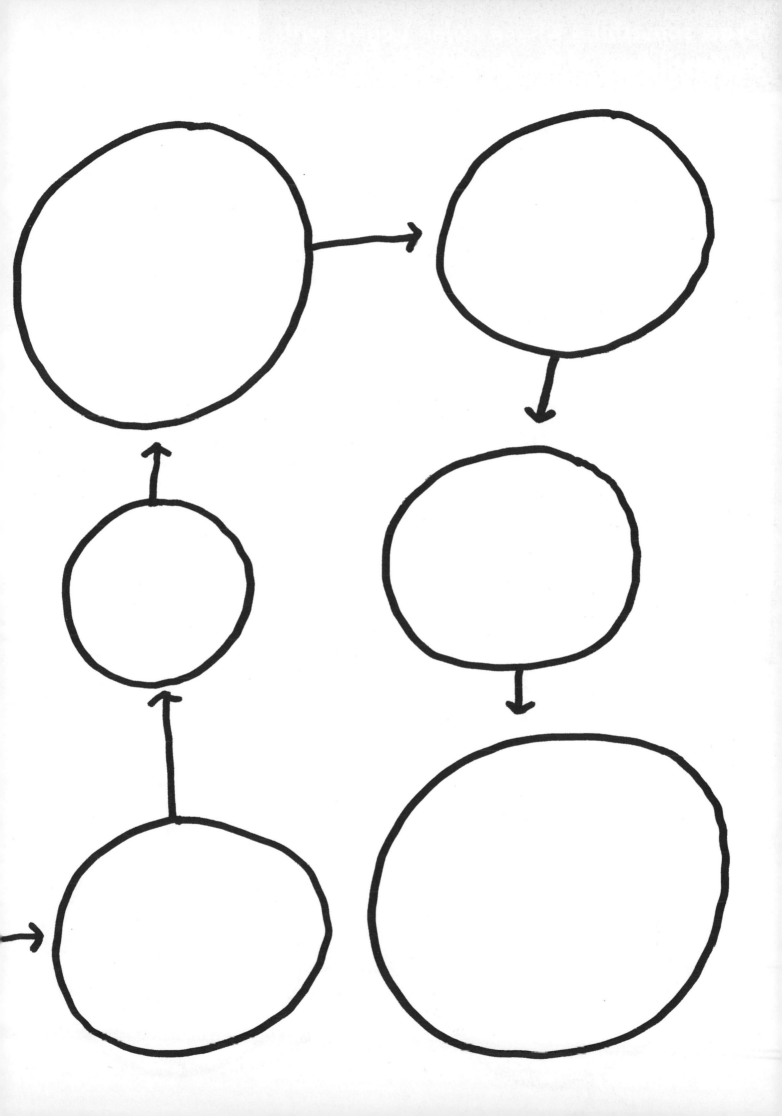

Draw something whose name begins with the last letter of the thing before it.

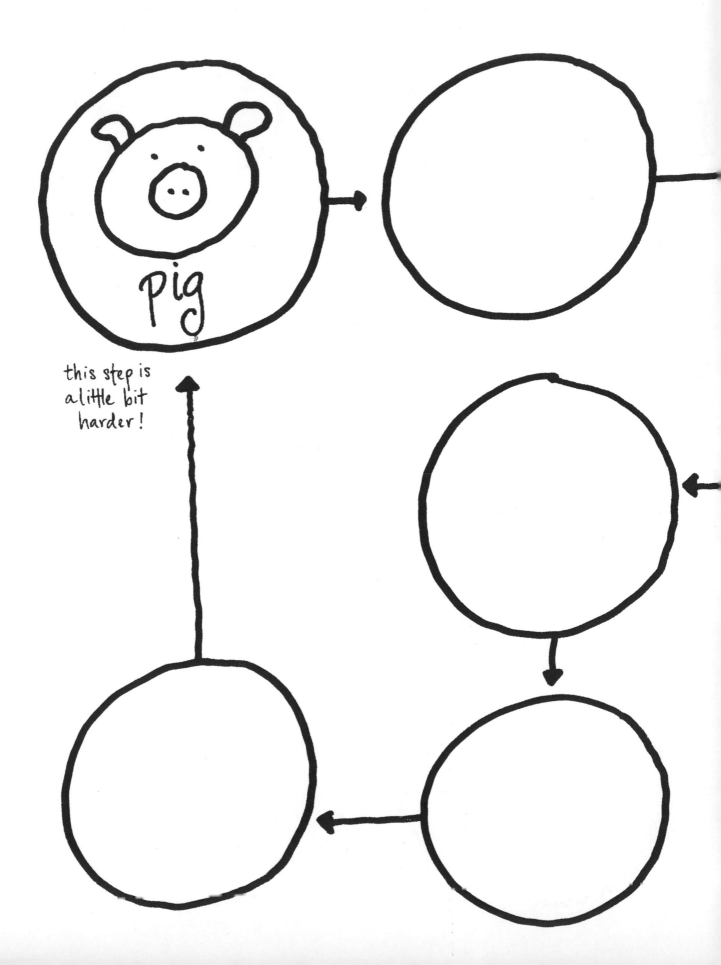

pig

this step is
a little bit
harder!

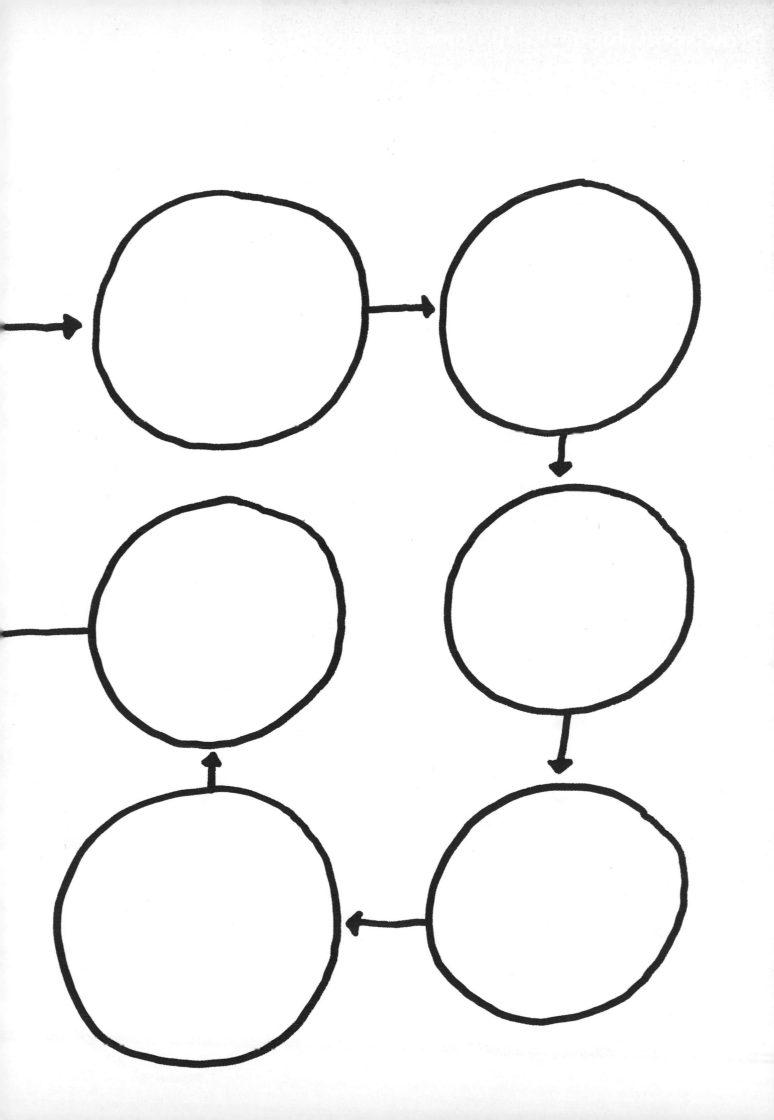

What are these cans spraying?

Shaving cream? Whipped cream? Jellyfish?

NON
FLUORO
GAS

Net. 43c

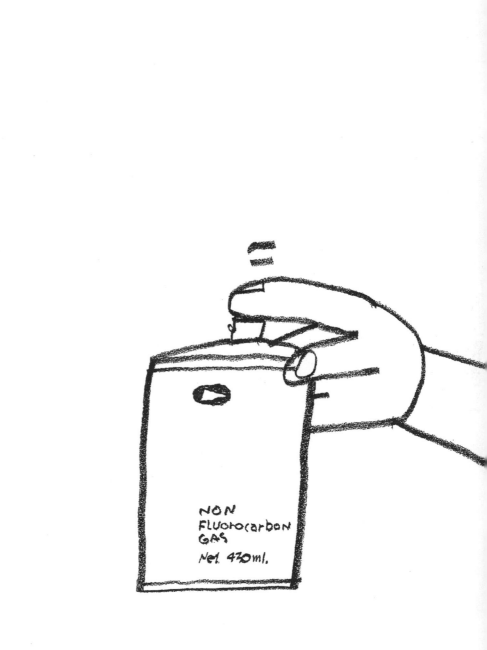

Draw faces that match these names.

Beth	Jo	Molly
Taro	Tracy	Jack
Cathleen	Brenden	Victoria

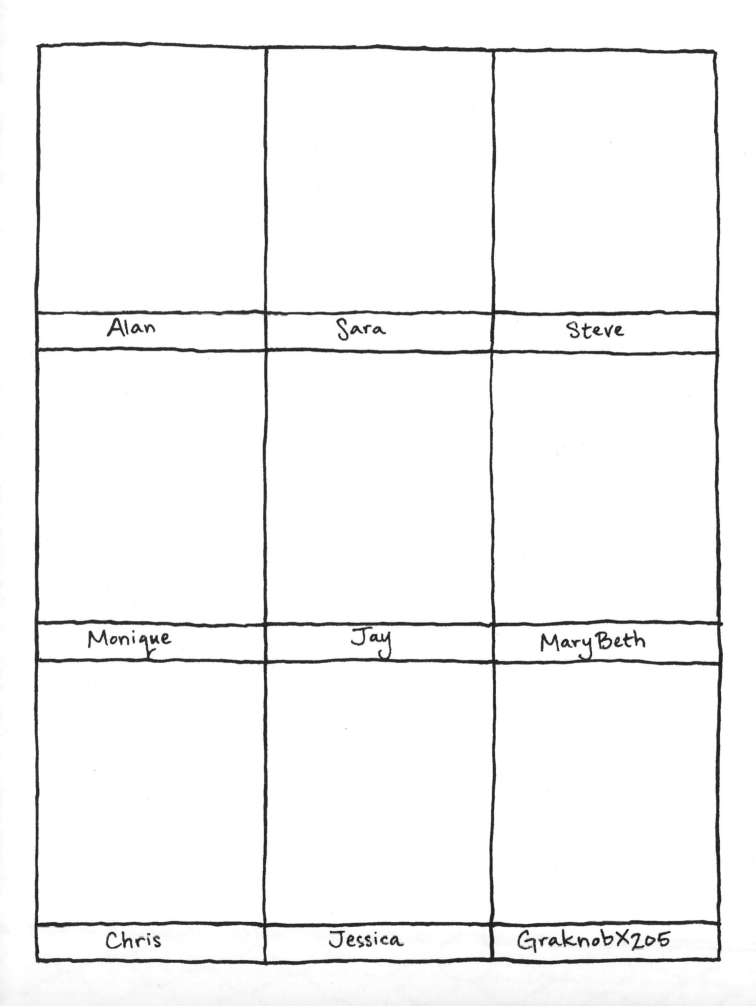

Alan	Sara	Steve
Monique	Jay	Mary Beth
Chris	Jessica	GraknobX205

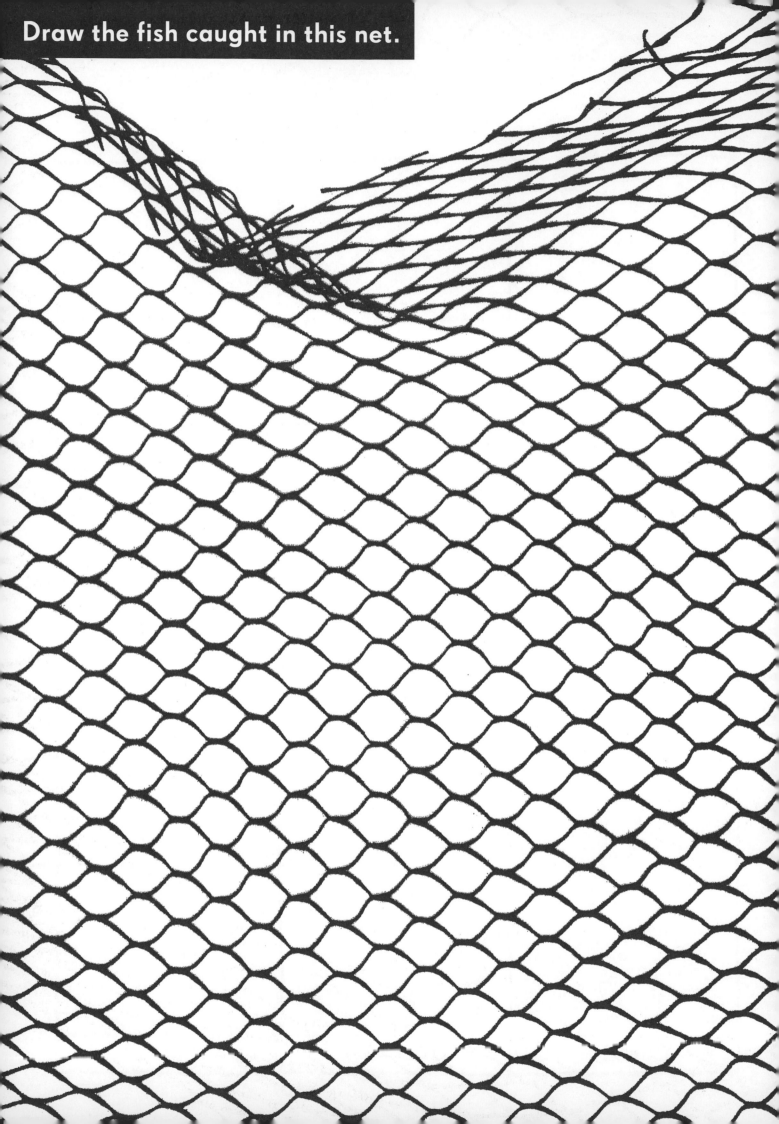

Draw the fish caught in this net.

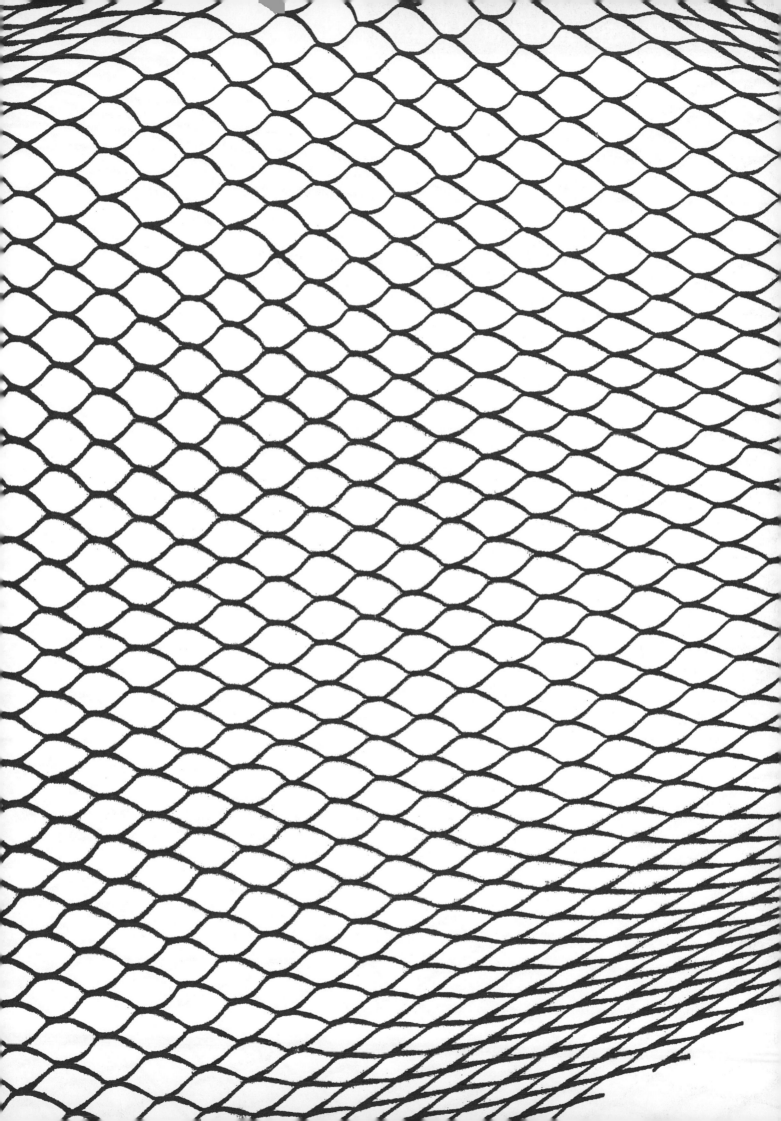

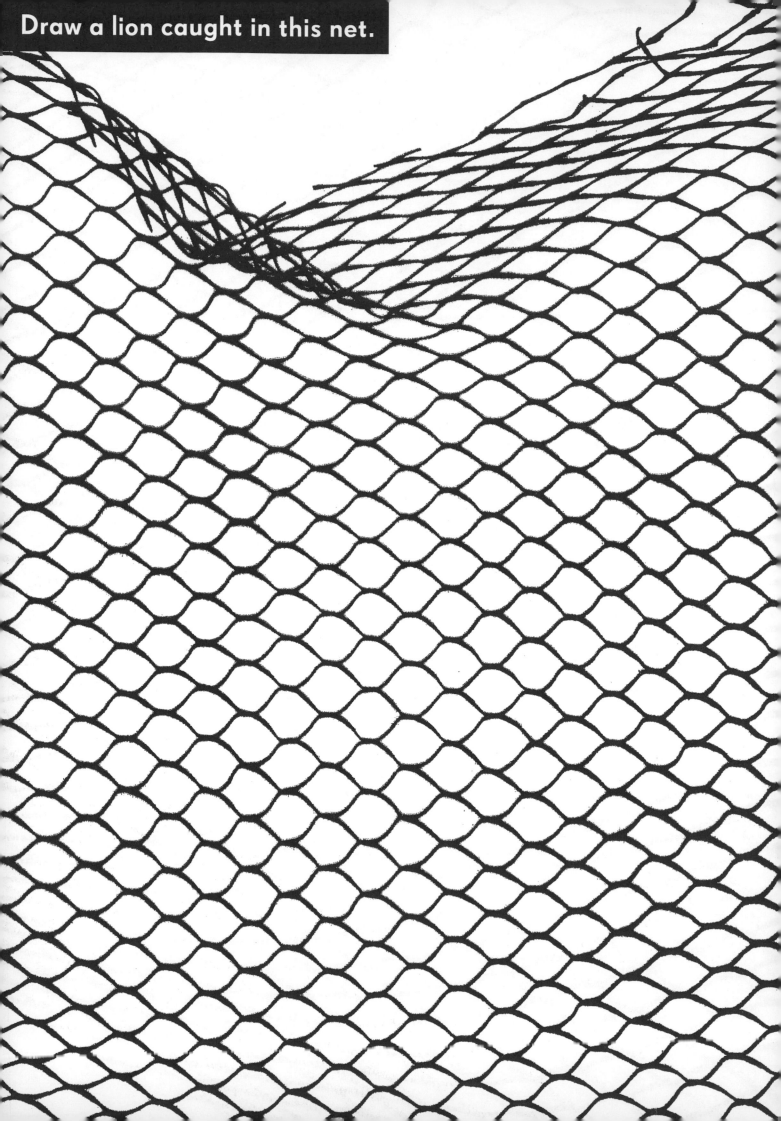

Draw a lion caught in this net.

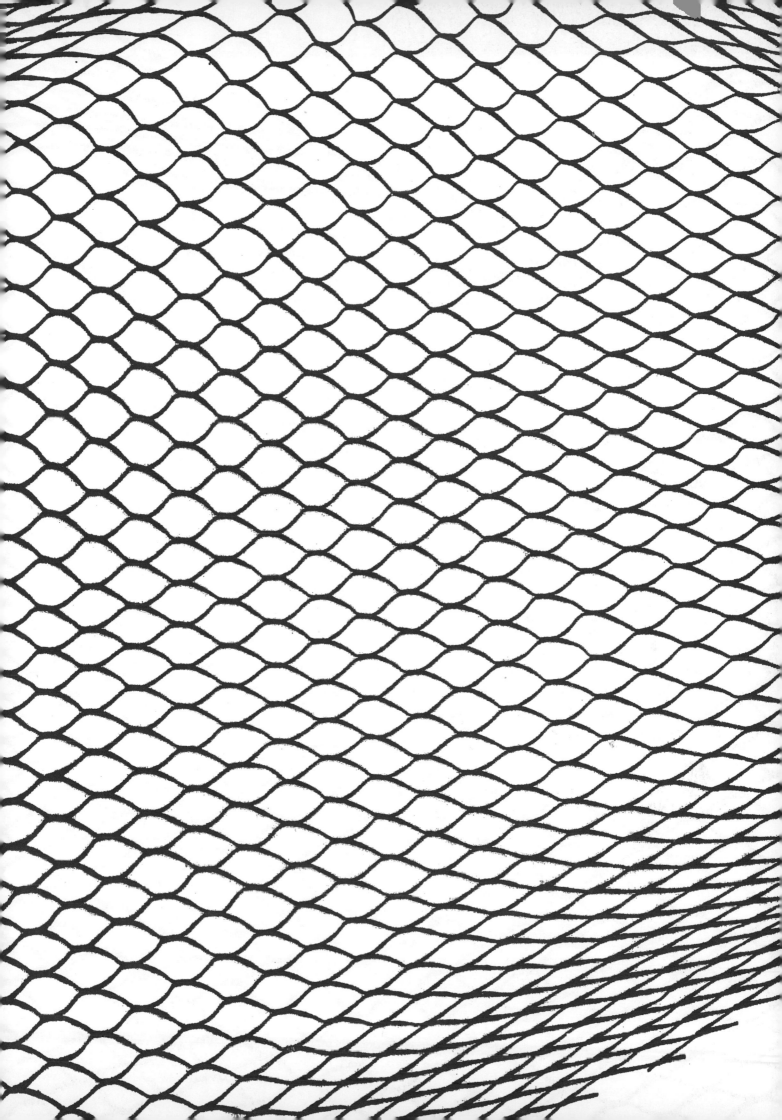

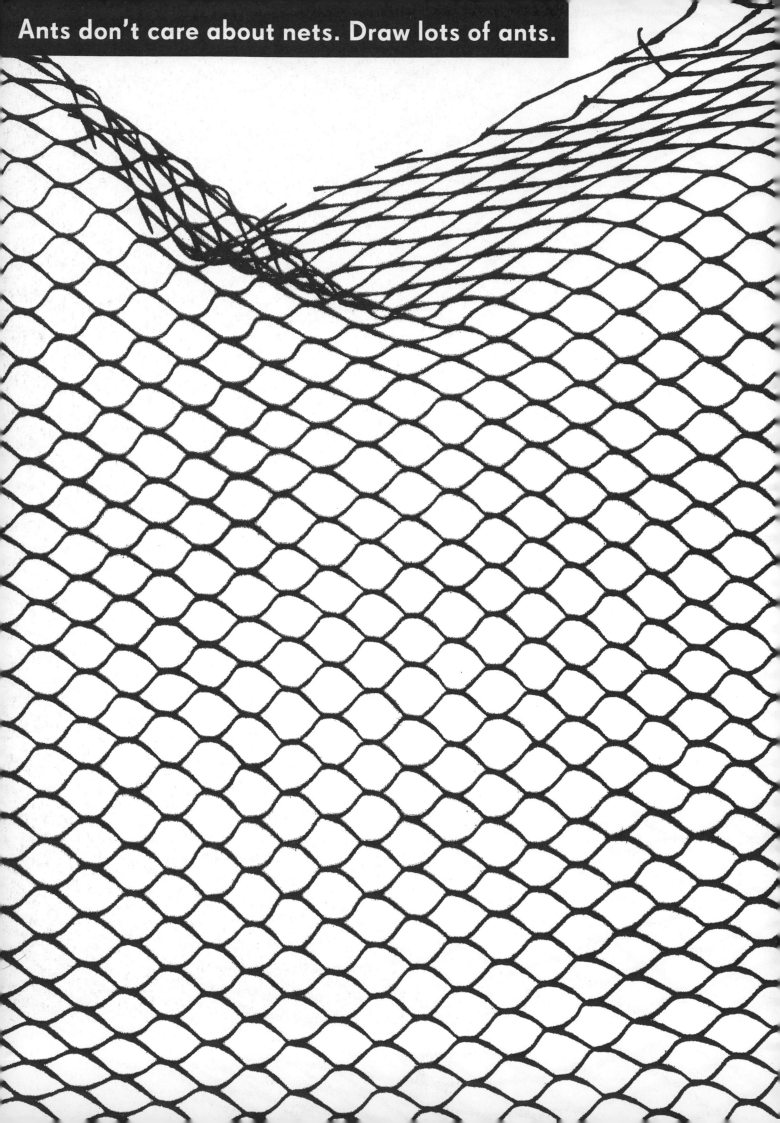

Ants don't care about nets. Draw lots of ants.

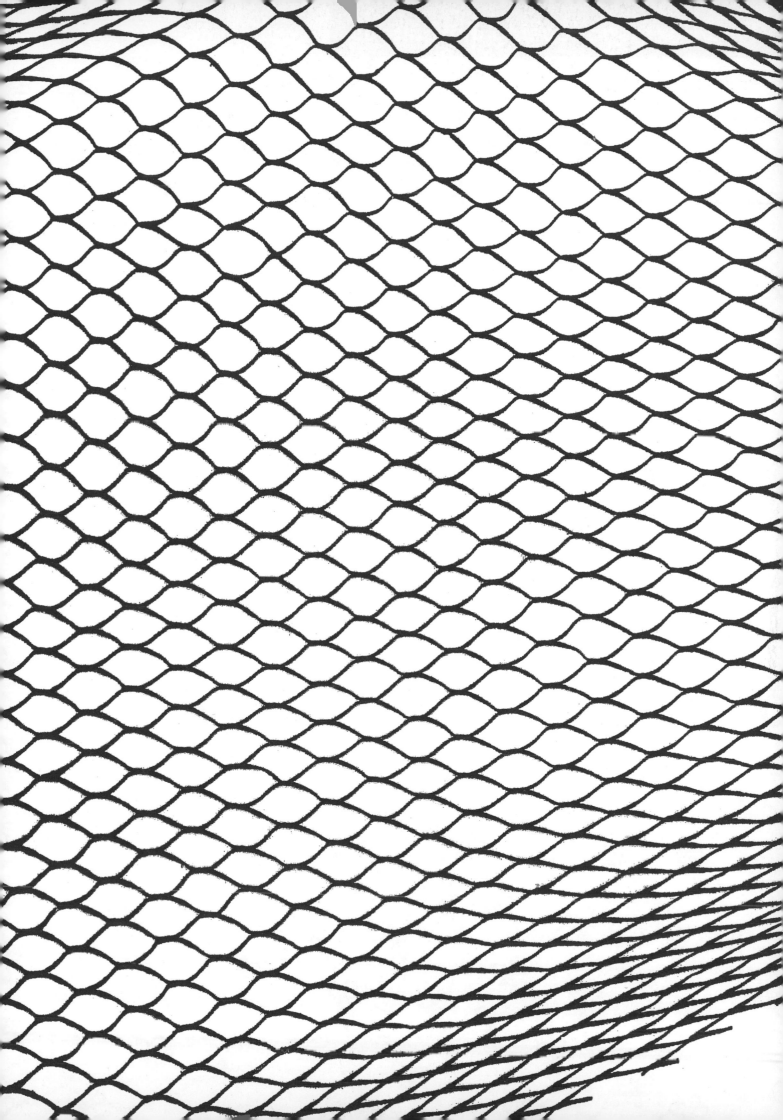

Find the mean-looking mosquitoes.

You can light up these lightbulbs by drawing the electrical wires between the batteries and the bulbs.

Help them paint the wall.

Make it all the same color if you can!

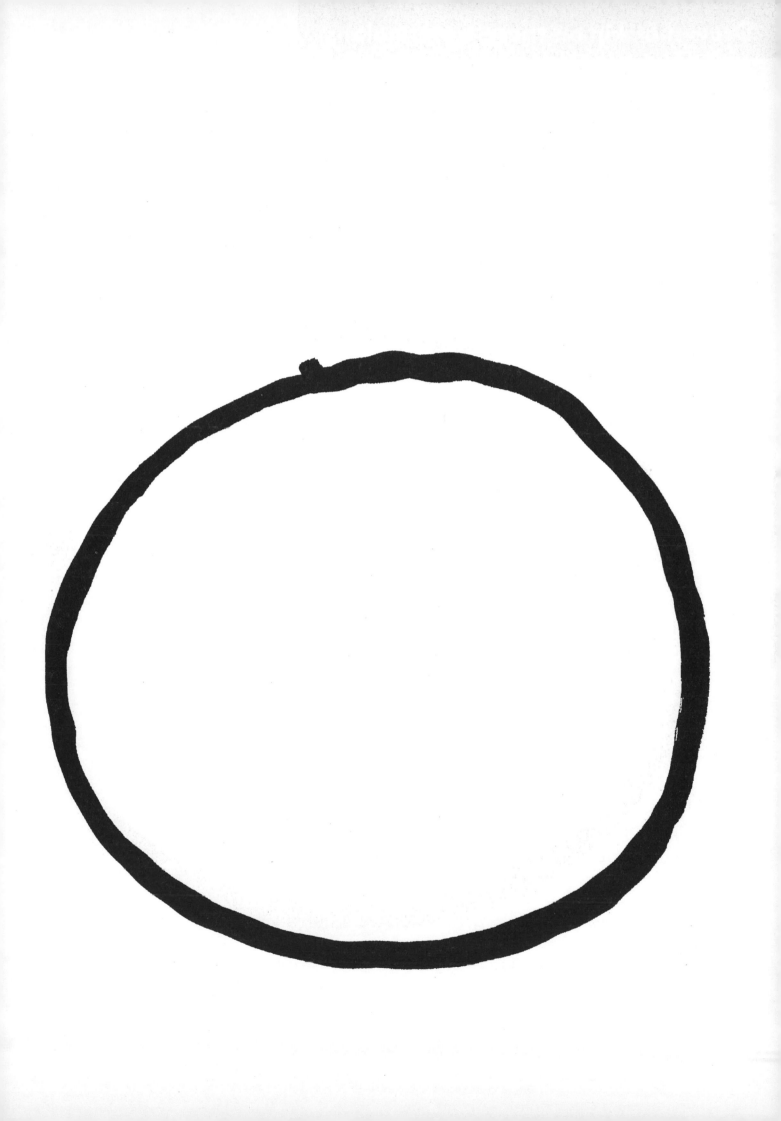

These are watermelons cut in half. Color the insides.

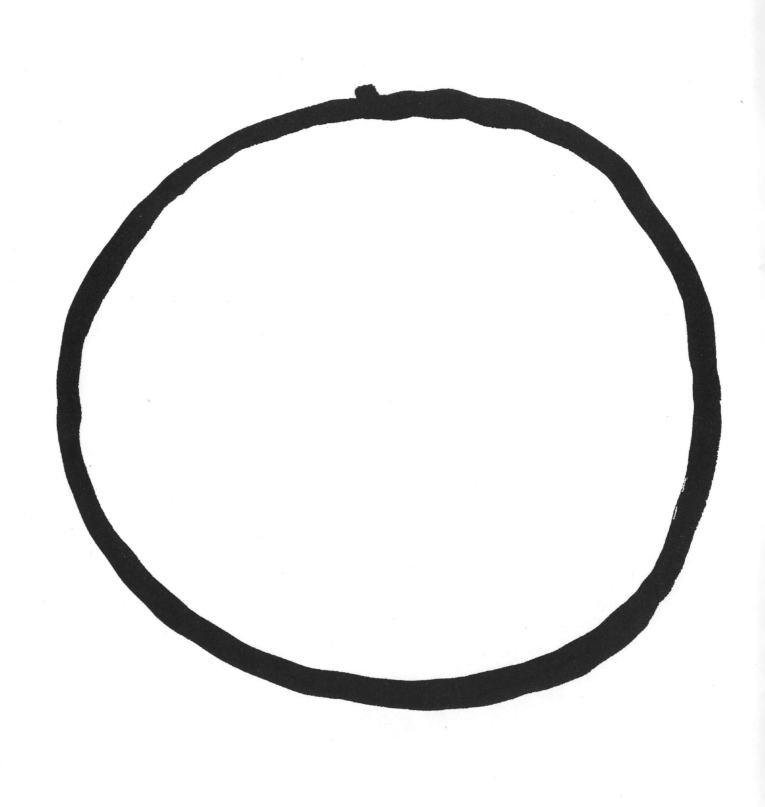

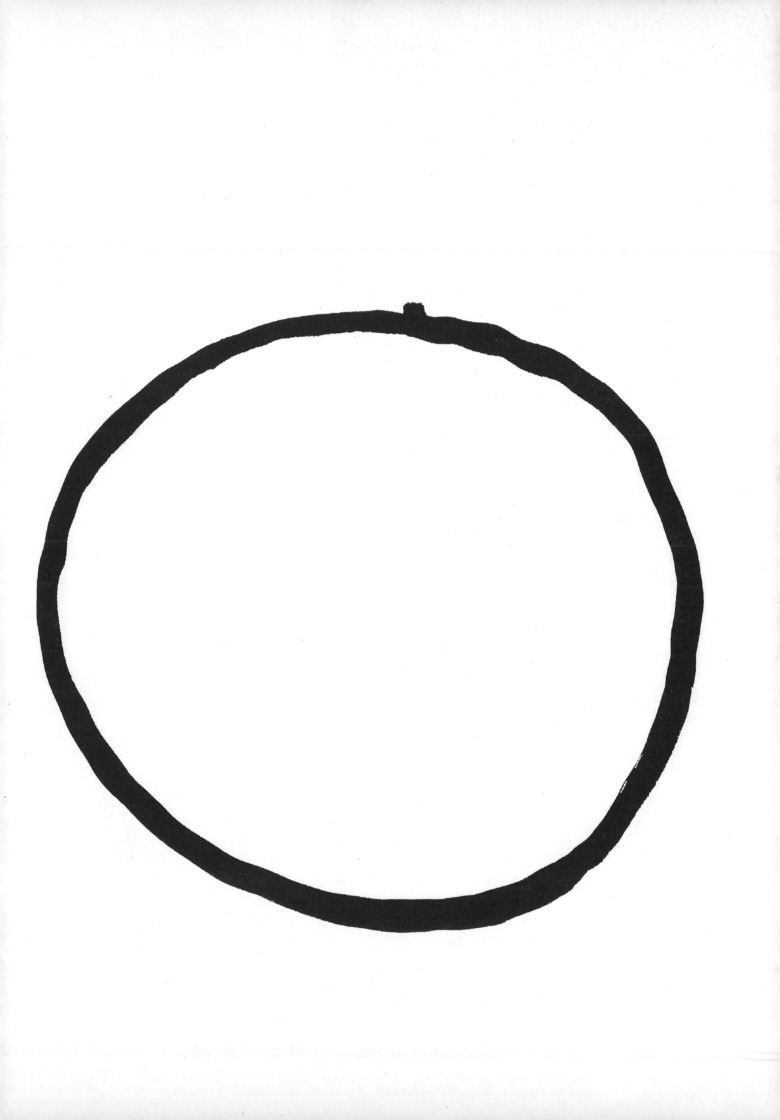

Make a nice snowman.

Which one of them is laughing harder?

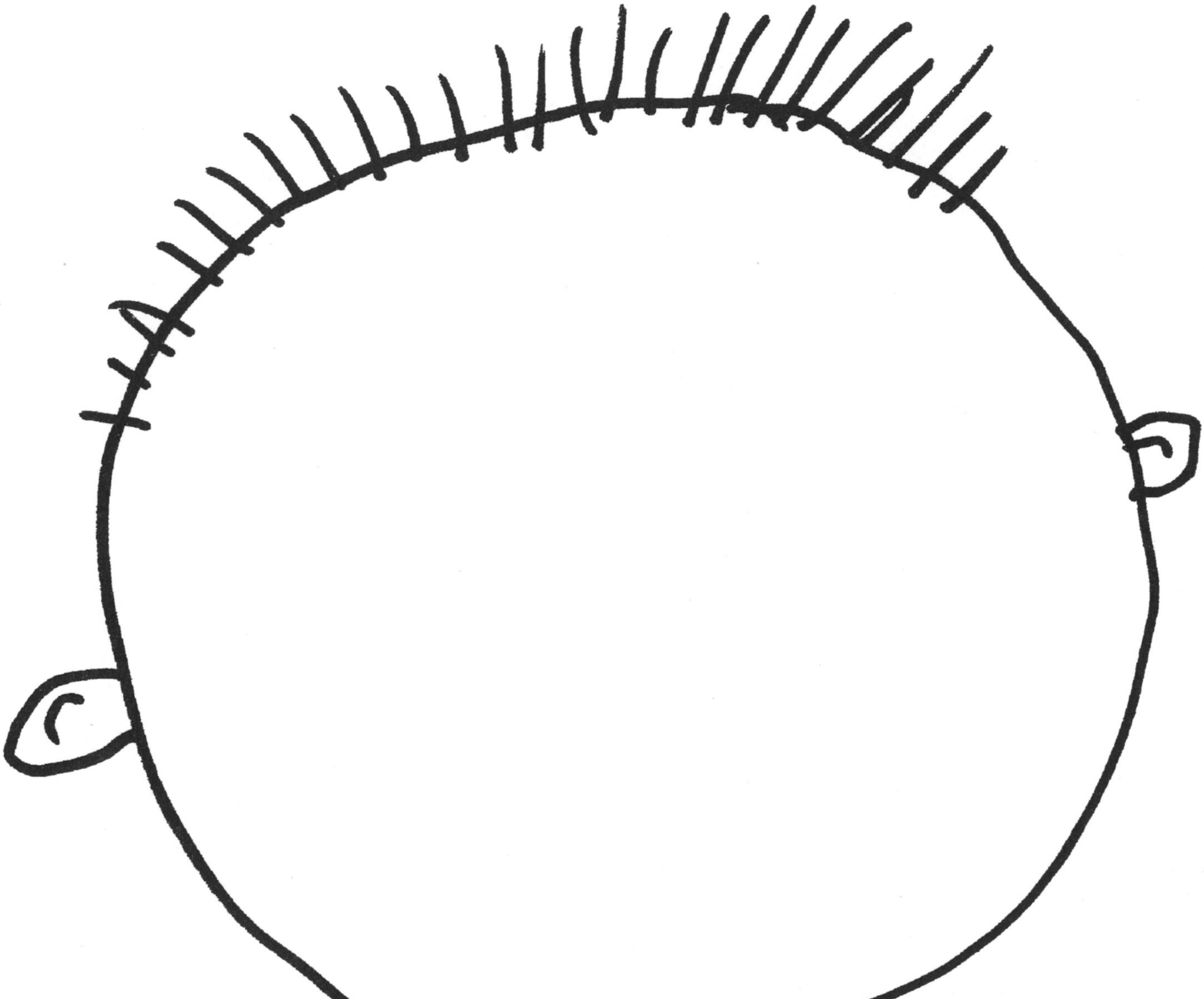

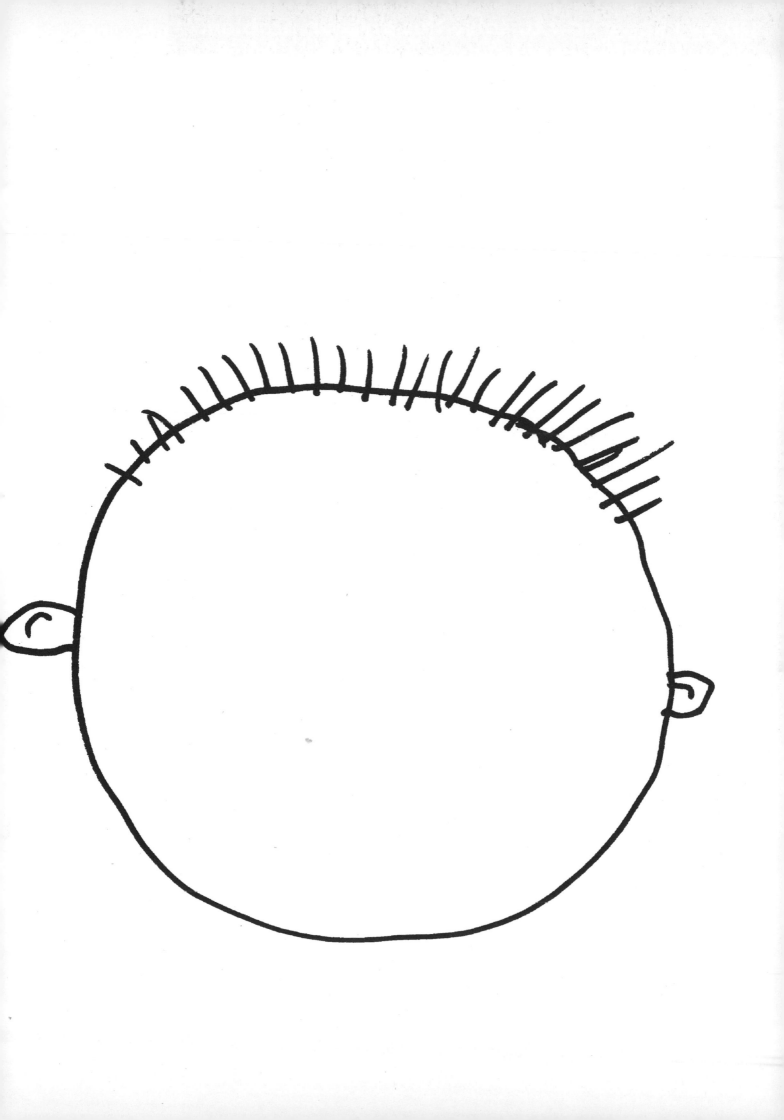

$$46 \overline{\smash{\big)}\,16790}$$

Each right answer is worth 5 points.

1. $15 + 18 = 23$
2. $30 - 6 = 14$
3. $20 + 20 + 15 = 85$
4. $30 - 3 = 27$
5. $50 \div 2 = 24$
6. $23 + 8 = 41$
7. $35 \times 2 + 1 = 71$
8. $8 + 2 + 9 + 2 + 4 = 22$
9. $5 - 2 + 4 + 2 + 8 = 3$
10. $600 \div 30 = 50$
11. $200 \div 10 + 2 - 1 = 21$
12. $(5 + 38) \times 2 = 88$

13. $20 \div 3 = 7.1$
14. $9 + 5 \times 12 \div 3 = 29$
15. $4 + 5 = 9$
16. $9 - 2 = 7$
17. $6 + 3 = 10$
18. $10 - 2 - 2 = 5$
19. $18 \div 3 = 8$
20. $900 + 25 - 23 + 6 - 4 = 903$

number of right answers:	total number of points:

What do you think they are talking about? Write their words.

The End

F_5; D_2; I_7; $D6$; G_3; B_4; A_3; I_1; J_4; $E8$; J_5; G_9; I_3; E_4; E_2; (Have you figured out what it is?) $B8$; $I8$; G_7; H_1; B_2; G_1; $B6$; $E6$; C_2; I_2; (You'd better hurry) F_1; $D8$; F_9; $C6$; C_4; $J6$; I_9; A_7; (Almost there) H_9; $C8$; D_4; (Hurray! You finished!) H_5.

Now add some whiskers!

	1	2	3	4	5	6	7	8	9
A									
B									
C									
D									
E									
F									
G									
H									
I									
J									
K									
L									

This time, it's not a picture. I7; F6; H1; D9; C3; K4; L6; A6; A8; E5; H3; C1; H9; J8; D5; L1; E3; K5; K9; A2; H5; E9; I1; J9; H4; I3; F1; C9; J5; L3; A7; C7; D7; (Can you guess what this is going to be?) F5; H7; G1; A3; L5; F9; J7; K1; D3; A9; A4; C5; L4; F4; L9; L7; F8; B9; (Looks strange, doesn't it?) D1; F3; I8; I9; B1; C6; K3; E1; L2; J1; G9; (And now, for the finishing touch) A1.

It's a maze! Find your way out! (First, add some obstacles to make it harder.)

	1	2	3	4	5	6	7	8	9
A									
B									
C									
D									
E									
F									
G									
H									
I									
J									
K									
L									

Write how each person is feeling.

Pack these fish very carefully.

What will you pack them in? Ice?
Tin cans? Suitcases?

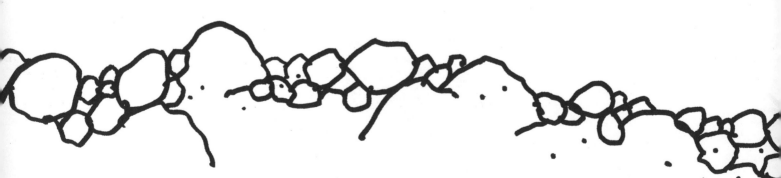

Draw each child's parents.

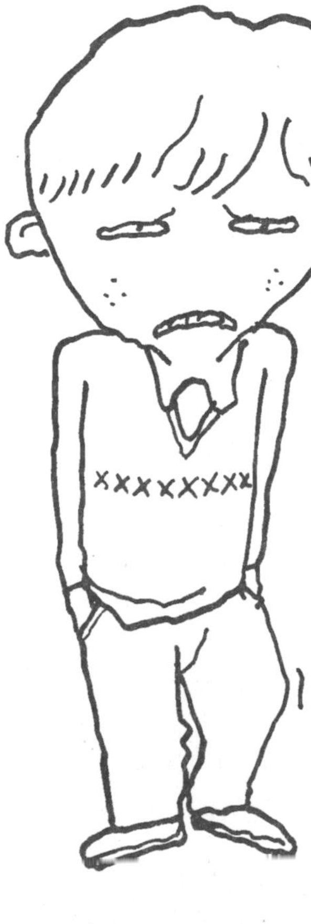

Some of these sunbathers have tans, but others have sunburns. You have to decide which is which.

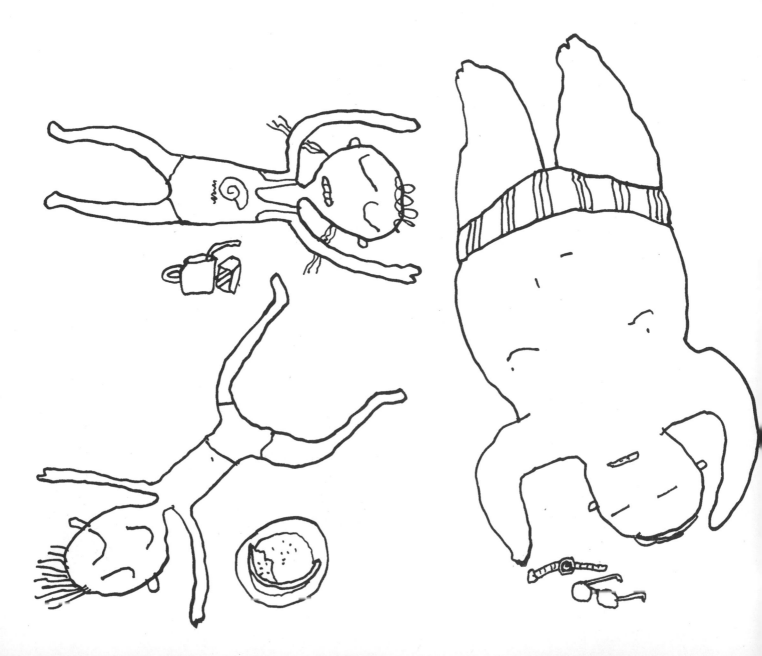

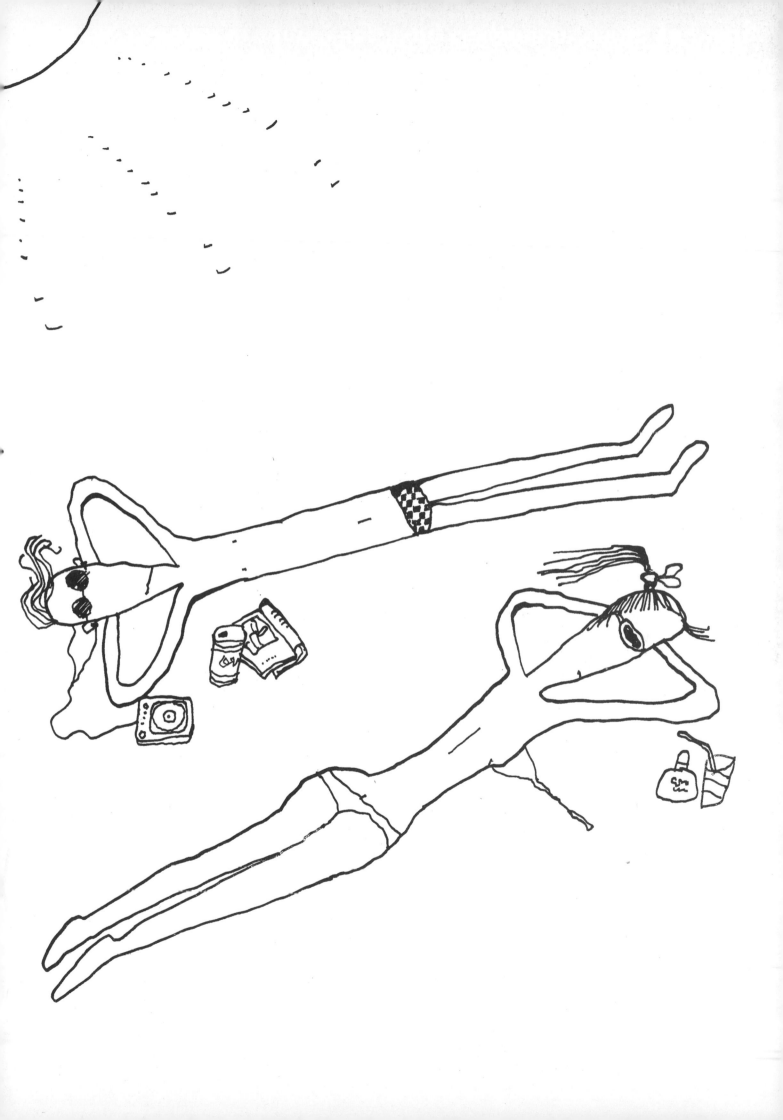

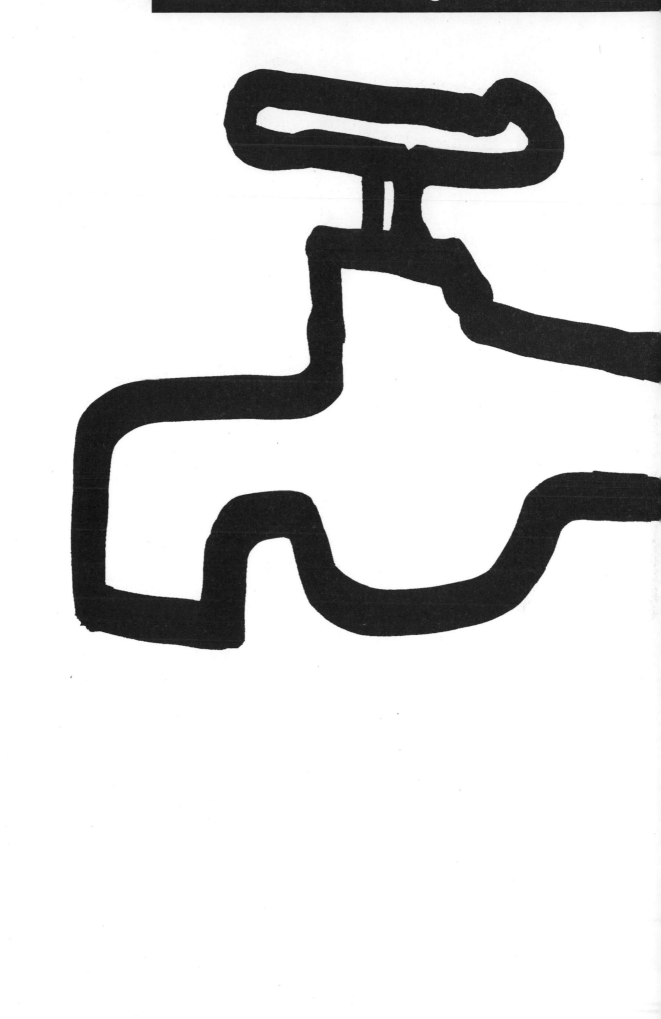

Can you draw ice for these penguins to walk on?

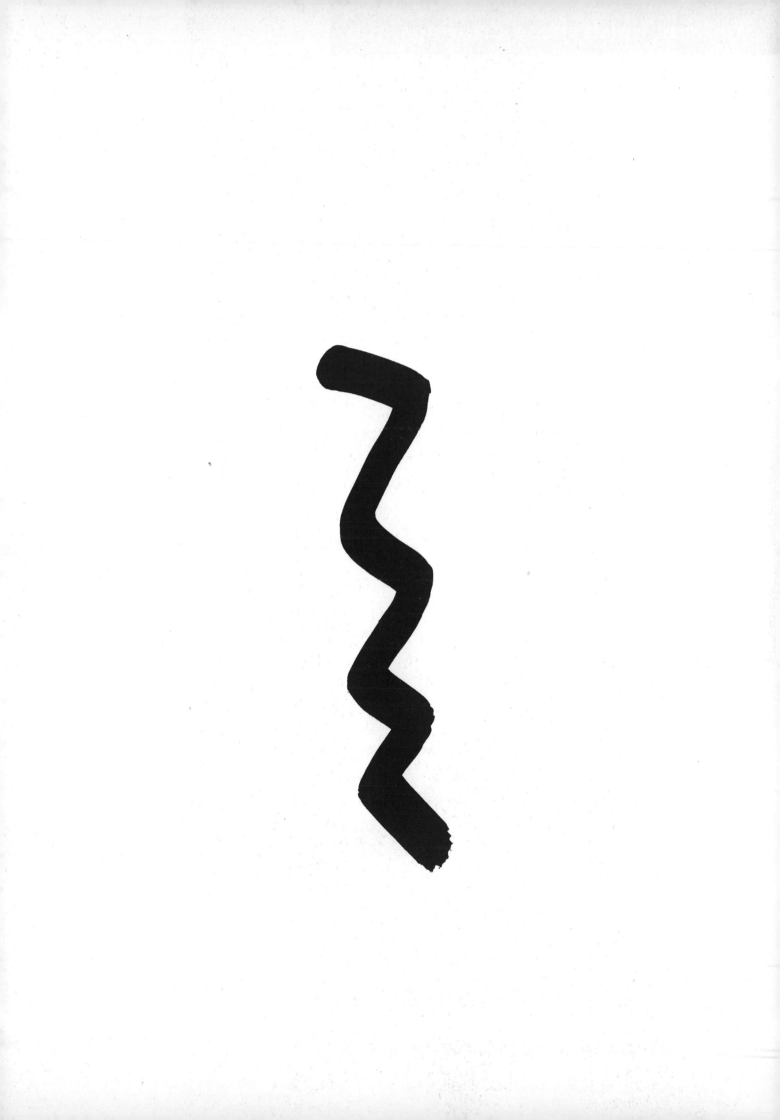

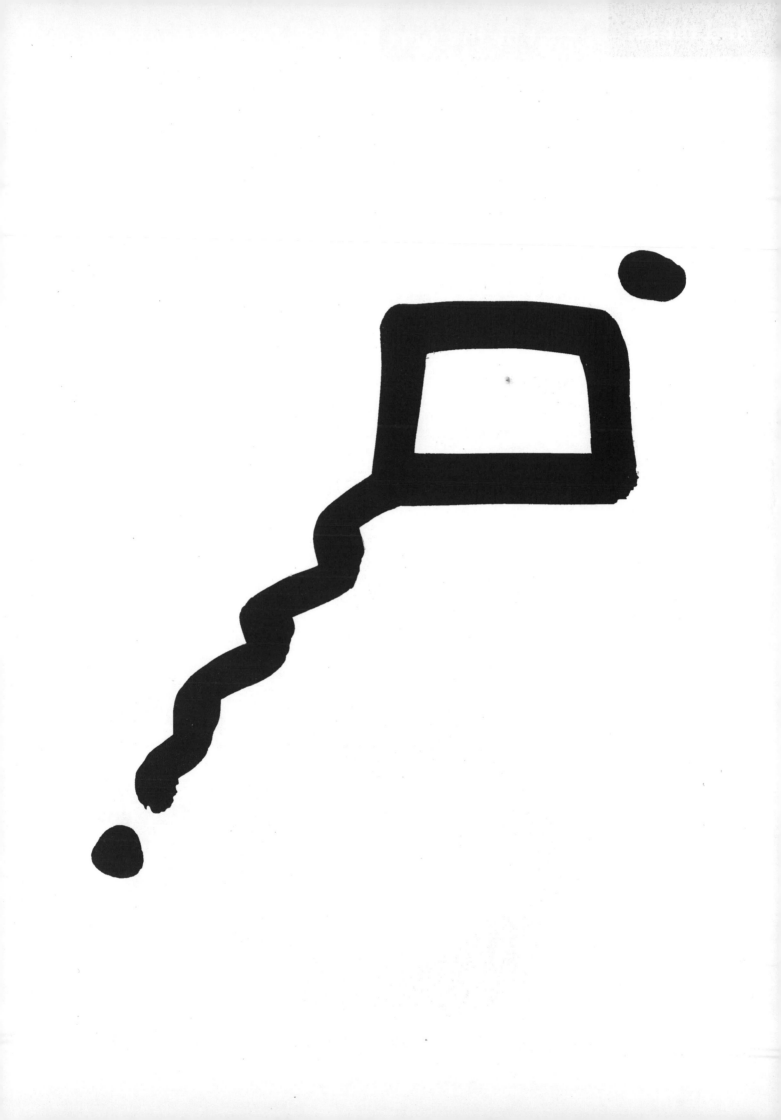

What kind of music do you think is coming out of these speakers?

**Here are two music boxes.
Draw the songs they're playing.**

The sun is setting behind these mountains.

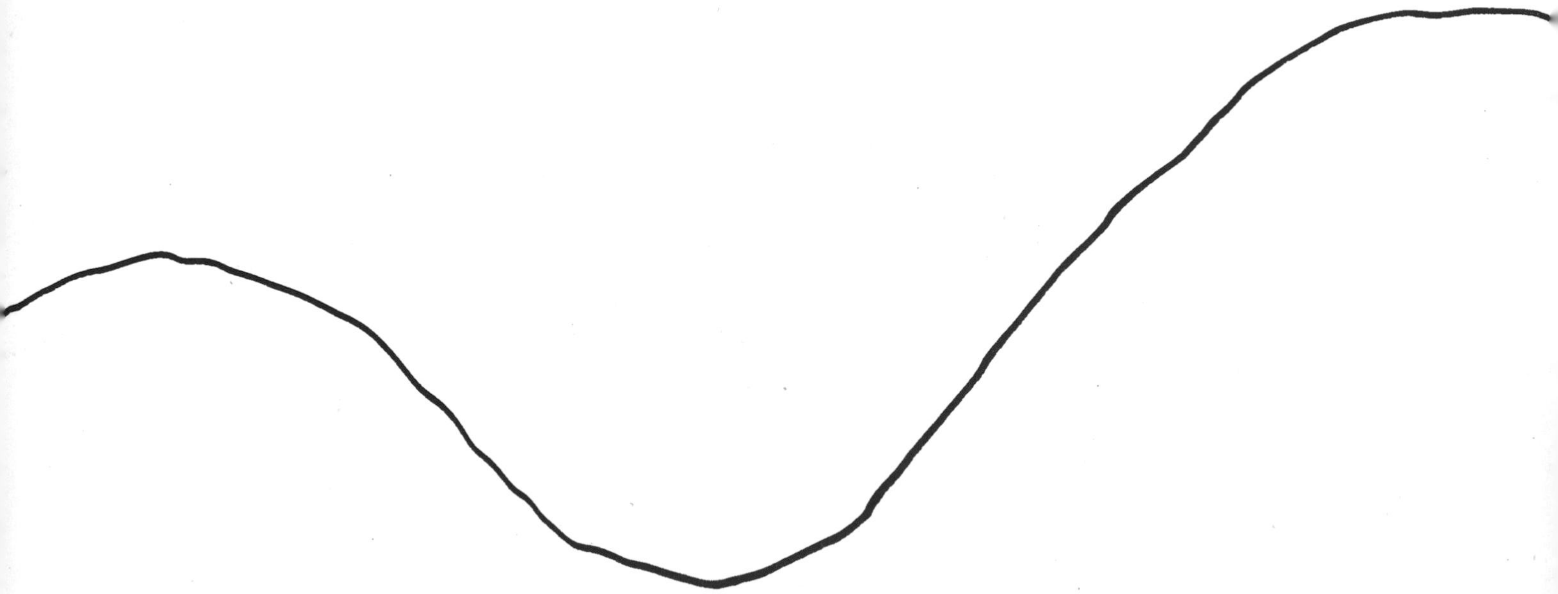

Now, the sun is rising from behind these mountains.

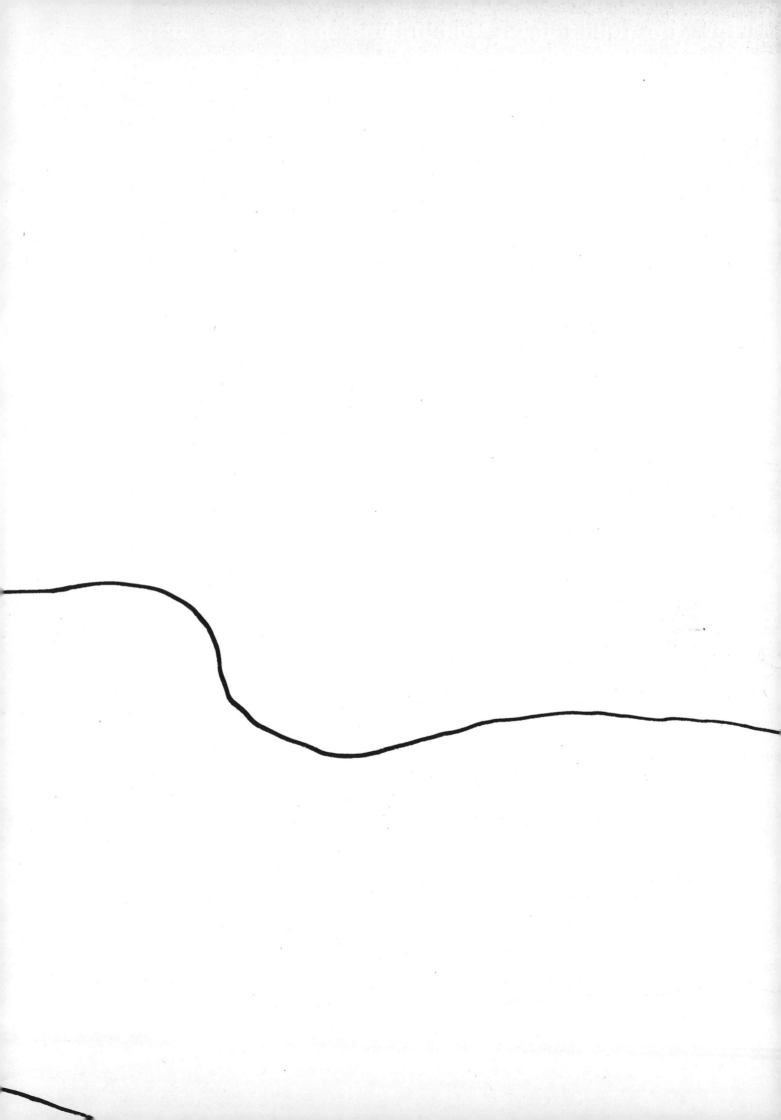

Draw rain falling in the ocean.

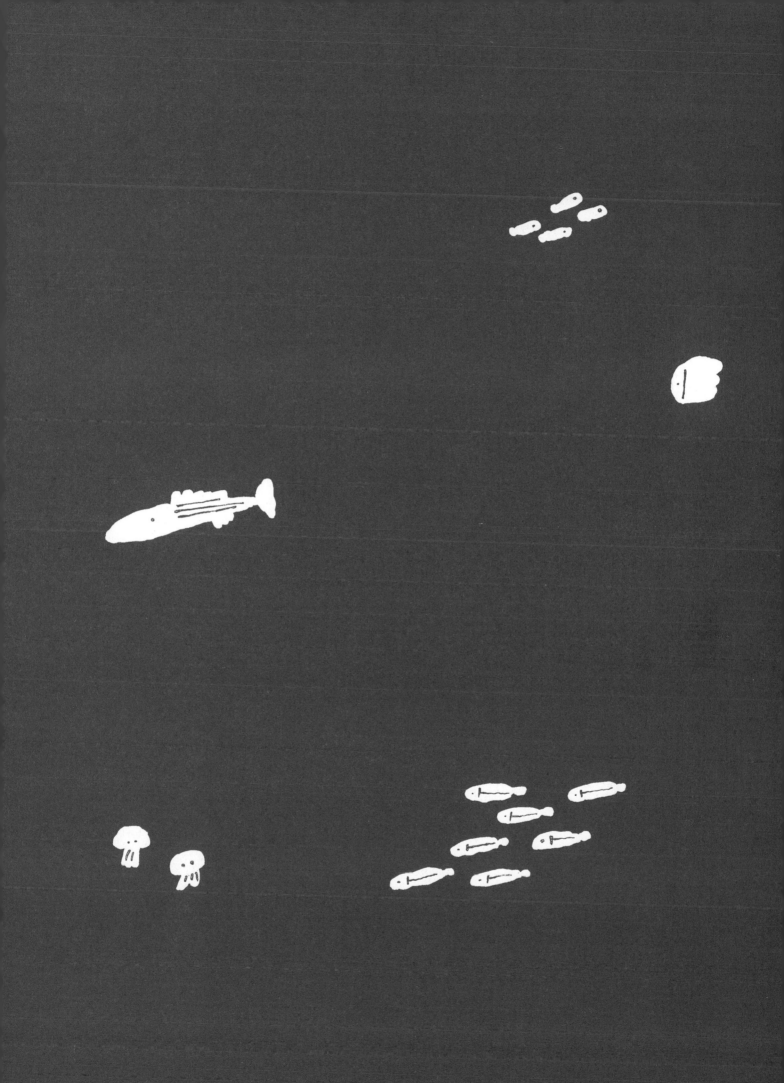

blue whale

manta ray

**Now, you're at the zoo.
Draw the animals whose names appear below.**

lynx

brown bear

palm tree

POW!

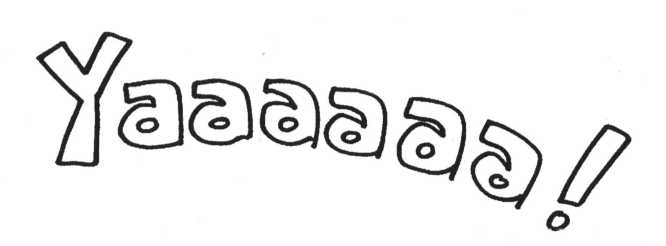

ticatica ticatica ticatica ticatica ticatica

poof! poof!

GRRRRRRRR!

chiiinng—!!

BANG!

ting ting ting!

BOOM! BOOM!

CRASH!!

VROOM, VROOOM, VROOOM!

whooo

tok! tok!

tok!
tok!

tok!
tok!

tok!
tok!

ah!

What do you think can be making these noises?

Huh?

These dinosaurs are trying to scare each other.

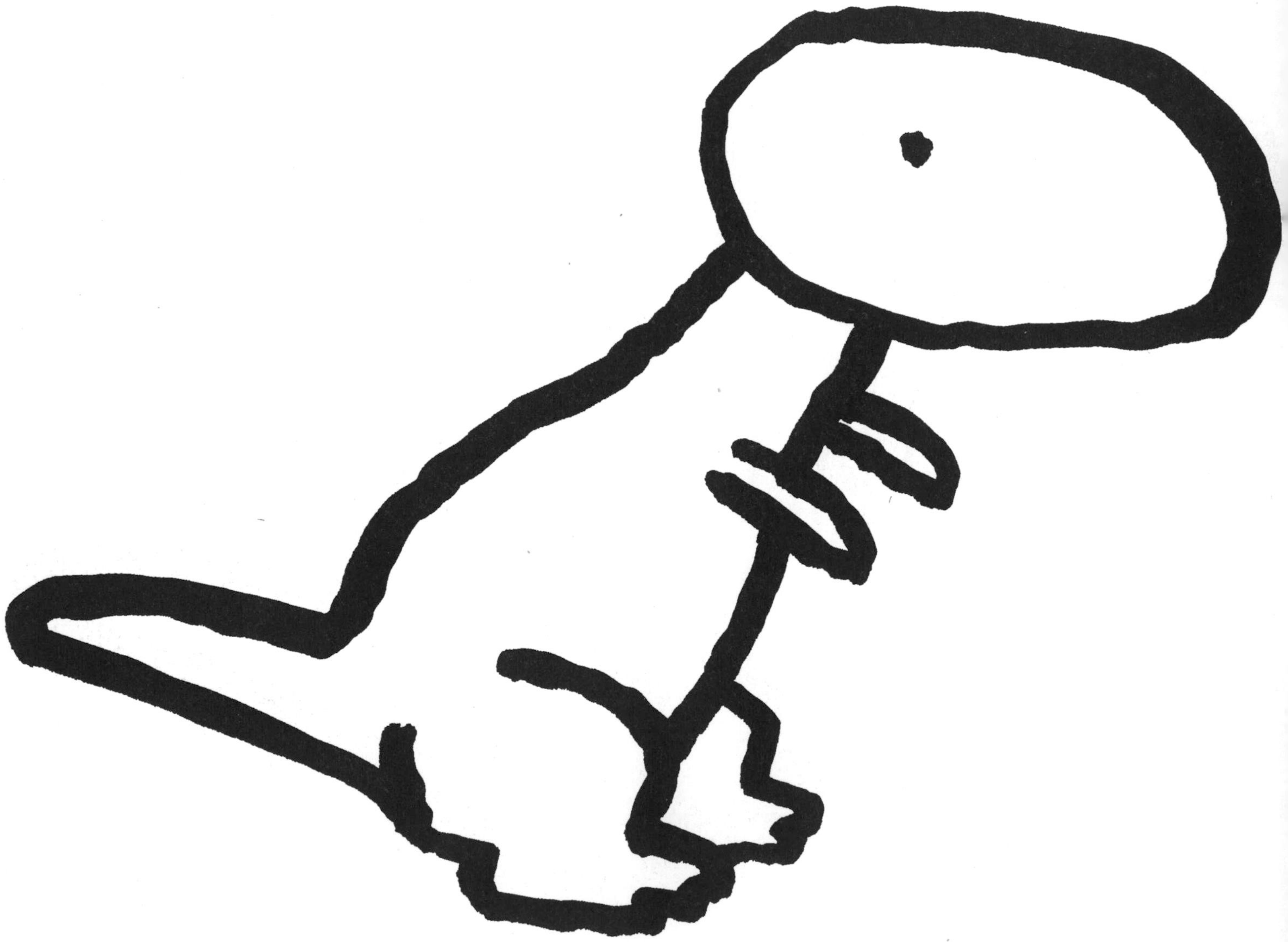

Word search. Circle all the words you can find.

Look for words from left to right and right to left, top to bottom, bottom to top, and even diagonally. We found 242. Can you find that many?

M	E	N	E	C	K	E	B	E	N	T	S	H	E	S	O	O	E
I	T	O	C	A	X	L	O	N	G	F	H	E	P	O	O	L	S
C	A	N	A	E	R	T	N	A	C	I	I	B	O	I	R	O	N
D	O	N	T	K	L	D	E	H	I	S	P	N	H	A	T	P	E
W	P	E	O	W	E	S	T	Y	Z	H	E	O	T	R	E	E	A
S	I	L	E	N	O	O	P	E	N	O	N	O	A	S	O	X	R
L	N	E	O	R	A	N	G	J	E	L	P	N	X	J	A	R	L
A	K	M	U	A	B	A	E	A	S	P	O	E	I	K	N	R	P
H	E	O	A	I	R	J	B	P	C	C	U	P	M	I	C	E	Y
P	E	N	Z	L	A	I	R	A	I	L	B	F	I	S	H	E	N
U	P	K	E	O	D	M	E	N	U	H	S	O	C	E	L	L	V
B	E	H	E	N	E	N	Q	L	E	G	T	O	V	B	O	A	D
O	N	C	U	V	N	Z	O	O	M	O	V	D	P	O	W	A	X
O	A	H	A	N	D	C	T	E	N	O	W	E	E	X	M	T	E
K	T	W	Z	E	Q	U	I	Z	L	S	C	S	D	K	E	S	P
D	E	R	E	S	V	A	E	X	I	T	R	E	E	L	L	Q	E
Y	O	E	A	T	U	I	E	U	W	H	O	I	J	X	O	H	T
Z	O	G	E	O	O	S	G	A	O	L	Q	U	E	E	N	L	X
E	C	P	I	N	E	X	E	C	Z	H	V	B	O	O	T	S	B
N	Q	G	F	E	M	E	M	A	O	A	B	Y	B	O	Y	K	I
V	A	S	E	P	I	N	G	N	N	E	S	N	E	T	A	J	T
P	R	H	J	I	L	E	P	Z	O	Z	X	M	A	S	O	F	E
B	E	P	K	G	E	O	D	E	B	E	W	A	X	O	X	E	R
Y	E	L	L	O	W	N	C	O	W	B	G	I	R	L	V	I	C

Word search. Circle all the words you can find.

Look for words from left to right and right to left, top to bottom, bottom to top, and even diagonally. We found 56. Maybe you'll find more!

```
S G S A P E B O W F H T I B B I R Q
P L O P V U A L Z S L F T O R W O U
L E V Y P H R Q X W F O M P H R A I
A R A W O N K R U I K T O O S G R S
T H U D P L V O N S U G O Y A N J P
W T G Z V I E S F H E S B V R O O M
U C R A C K L E G E H A G P C I J U
T H E I Y K Q U H I S S N H Z C O H
V S Q U E A K E E L K N I T N R L T
H Y U K Z P G D G K R N D O M U K Y
E O A I S O O Z U L N L C O O N N L
E F C U L W O R G T D I P H M C I K
K A K W A U Q S E G N I O B O H L H
C D C H S C Y U N B F N H A G E C G
I P L N K N S M A C K R H R I E Q U
L F A V X T O I B G C E U O E P L B
C R M X W S A R O B W N J R D H R L
L B C T H U N K T F T O C I Y J U M
W L Y K A B L O O I E S W K P Y S O
J A M H P M A J L Z Y C R O A K A O
Z M Y P R I H C K Z Q U F P N Z M R
H E L T T A R W O H S A L P S N D L
A O W B I P Q A R U W Y G A B U Z Z
L W O H Y K N I L P L U N K T G V K
```

Word search.

Look for words from left to right and right to left, top to bottom, bottom to top, and even diagonally. We found 57. Maybe you'll find more!

Top to bottom, bottom to top, right to left, any old direction.

2	6	3	9	5	0	2	2	4	3	8	9	0	8	1	4	6	5
3	7	8	5	0	1	2	4	0	8	9	1	2	3	3	4	5	9
9	8	7	3	2	8	6	5	5	4	1	6	5	6	0	1	7	6
1	5	0	1	3	4	7	1	3	6	3	2	4	4	7	6	5	9
6	4	5	3	6	8	2	6	6	0	5	3	5	0	5	3	0	1
0	1	1	6	3	5	2	1	2	6	4	6	4	5	4	2	4	7
6	2	5	9	1	2	6	1	1	1	4	3	2	7	8	1	2	9
3	6	4	6	8	2	6	3	2	4	5	6	7	0	2	3	4	4
1	3	5	0	2	4	8	6	9	2	3	0	3	6	6	5	2	6
8	1	1	2	0	3	4	7	6	4	5	1	2	2	4	3	0	2
9	1	2	9	2	3	0	3	6	4	8	1	2	9	2	4	3	1
1	0	3	5	2	3	1	3	4	3	2	3	6	7	7	3	2	0
2	5	1	2	4	1	8	2	2	8	5	0	5	9	1	6	1	1
1	6	8	2	5	8	4	6	1	5	7	3	7	8	2	3	5	1
4	2	6	2	1	2	3	0	2	7	1	2	6	5	2	8	3	2
6	8	2	4	1	3	1	2	1	1	1	2	4	4	5	2	6	7
3	2	1	5	5	7	3	4	1	9	8	1	0	8	6	7	1	2
7	6	3	6	8	2	2	8	6	3	1	0	2	9	3	4	0	0
1	3	9	2	4	1	0	6	5	3	7	5	4	1	8	1	1	4
1	2	3	6	5	2	1	2	2	5	2	8	3	4	0	2	2	3
2	5	0	2	9	8	4	5	3	10	2	1	5	6	2	7	5	9
9	0	0	0	3	6	0	1	9	1	1	0	6	4	1	5	8	4
1	3	2	1	0	5	2	1	4	2	8	2	5	2	6	7	1	2
0	4	4	2	5	7	3	0	5	6	1	7	2	3	6	2	2	0

Trace constellations in the night sky.

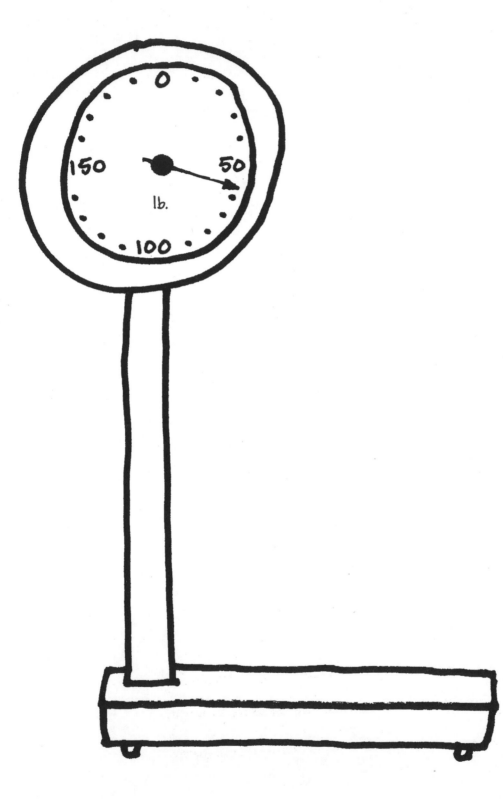

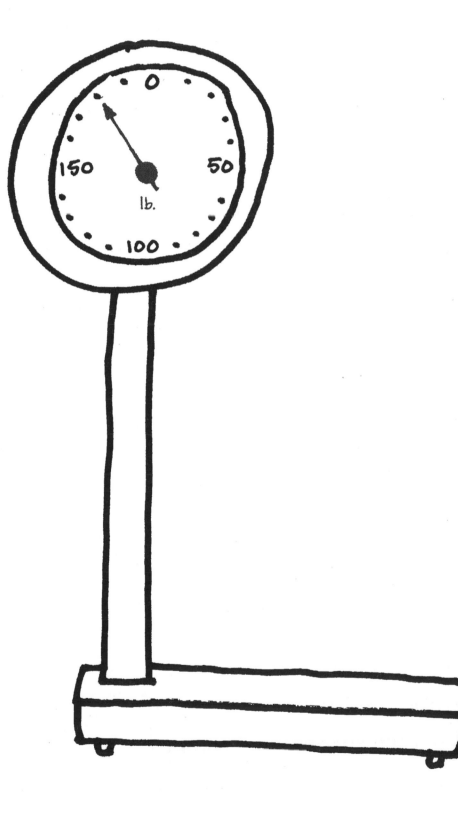

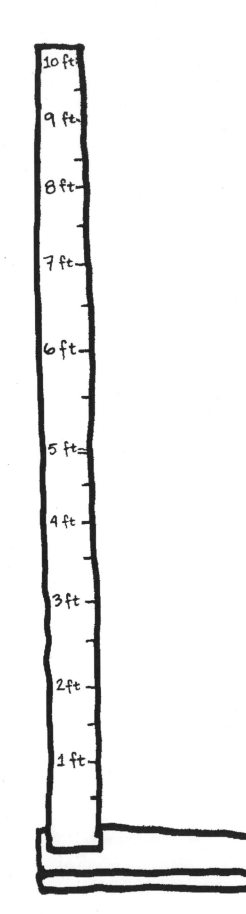

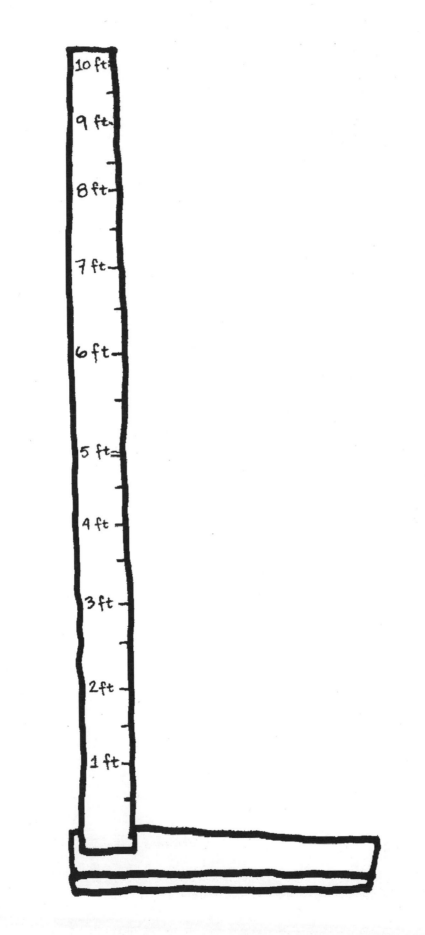

Do you want to make an 18-page book?

This time, you get to draw pictures to illustrate the story.
This page is the cover. The next page is the title page.

Super Patachawa

Story by Taro Gomi
Illustrations by _____

Astonishing, riveting, mysterious, shocking!
All-new adventures starring Super Patachawa.

Featuring illustrations by a talented young artist.

Brought to you by the Association of Paper Recyclers.

Doodles Books.

"Where are you going dressed like that?" asked the badger.
"To the beach," replied the fox.

"Why?" asked the badger.

"To play with this," answered the fox.

The badger looked. "What's that?" he asked.

"That," replied the fox, "is a Super Patachawa."

"A Super Patachawa? How does it work?"
 asked the badger.
"Come with me and you'll see," said the fox.

So the fox and the badger went to the beach together.

The fox started to play with the Super
Patachawa. It was amazing.
"Wow!" shouted the badger. He was
really impressed.

"Can I try?" asked the badger.
"Sure," answered the fox. "Go ahead."
The badger tried to play with the Super
Patachawa, but—

"Arg!" shouted the badger, because he couldn't get it to work.
"It takes practice," said the fox.

The badger seemed really frustrated.
"Look," said the fox, "I'll help you."
"Really?" exclaimed the badger. "That's great!"
And he was happy again.

So the badger stood next to the fox and watched him very carefully to see how to use the Super Patachawa.

"Wow! It's so cool!" cried the badger.

"Yep," agreed the fox.

And the fox was very proud of helping his friend.

They had a great time playing with the Super Patachawa. When night fell, they were still playing with it when suddenly . . .

Draw these animals' footsteps.

**This is all that's left of this cookie.
Draw the whole thing.**

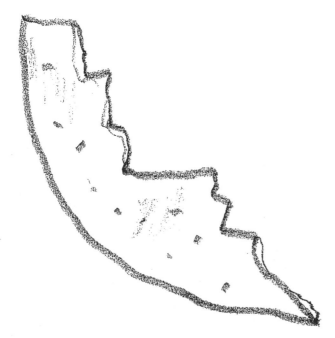

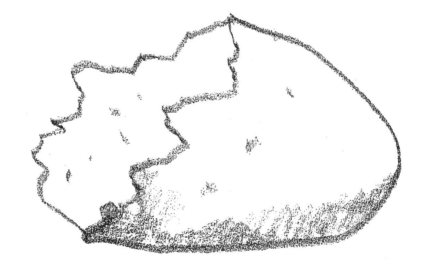

This is a pencil.
Draw someone drawing.

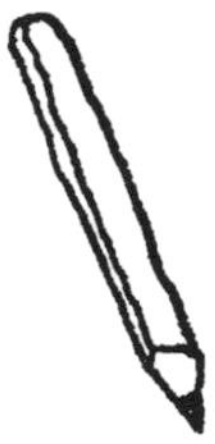

Draw something red.

Imagine a cushion in trouble . . .

and a chair that looks like it's bored.

Draw a huge nose.

Draw something entirely new—something that will make everyone ask, "What's that?"

Draw the Rabbit King.

Now draw whatever comes into your head.

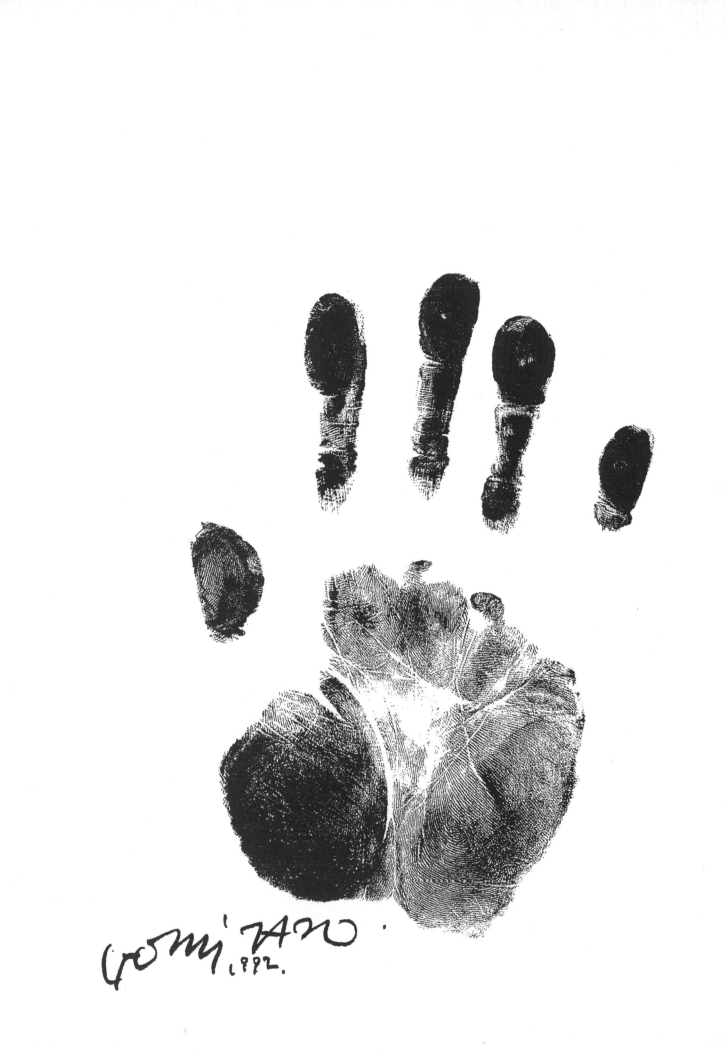